A
Taste-Berry™
Teen's Guide
To Setting &
Achieving
GOALS

A
Taste-Berry™
Teen's Guide
To Setting &
Achieving
GOALS

With contributions from teens for teens

Bettie B. Youngs, Ph.D., Ed.D.
Jennifer Leigh Youngs

**authors of the national bestselling
Taste Berries™ for Teens series and
Feeling Great, Looking Hot & Loving Yourself!**

**Health Communications, Inc.
Deerfield Beach, Florida**

www.hci-online.com

We would like to acknowledge the following publishers and individuals for permission to reprint the following material. (Note: The stories that were penned anonymously, that are public domain or were previously unpublished stories written by Bettie B. Youngs or Jennifer Leigh Youngs are not included in this listing. Also not included in this listing but credited within the text are those stories contributed or based upon stories by teens.)

Call Me "Dr. Santos," by Craig Santos. Reprinted with permission by publisher Health Communications, Inc., Deerfield Beach, Florida, from *More Taste Berries for Teens: A Second Collection of Inspirational Short Stories and Encouragement on Life, Love, Friendship and Tough Issues* by Bettie B. Youngs, Ph.D., Ed.D., and Jennifer Leigh Youngs. ©2000 Bettie B. Youngs, Ph.D., Ed.D., and Jennifer Leigh Youngs.

(Continued on page 297)

Library of Congress Cataloging-in-Publication Data

A taste-berry teen's guide to setting & achieving goals / [compiled by] Bettie
   B. Youngs, Jennifer Leigh Youngs.
        p.   cm.
   Summary: Stories, commentary, and advice by teens who relate their
experiences and share their ideas about setting and achieving goals.
   ISBN 0-7573-0040-5 (tp)
      1. Achievement motivation in adolescence. 2. Goal (Psychology) [1. Goal
(Psychology) 2. Success. 3. Youths' writings.] I. Youngs, Bettie B. II. Youngs,
Jennifer Leigh, date.
BF724.3.M65 T37 2002
158.1'0835—dc21

                                                              2002024143

Publisher: Health Communications, Inc.
            3201 S.W. 15th Street
            Deerfield Beach, Florida 33442-8190

R-09-02

Cover illustration and design by Larissa Hise Henoch
Inside book formatting by Dawn Von Strolley Grove

To:_____

...a definite "taste berry"!

From: _____

Also by Bettie B. Youngs, Ph.D.

Taste Berries for Teens #3: Inspirational Stories and Encouragement on Life, Love, Friends and the Face in the Mirror (Health Communications, Inc.)

A Taste-Berry Teen's Guide to Managing the Stress and Pressures of Life (Health Communications, Inc.)

More Taste Berries for Teens: A Second Collection of Inspirational Short Stories and Encouragement on Life, Love, Friendship and Tough Issues (Health Communications, Inc.)

Taste Berries for Teens Journal: My Thoughts on Life, Love and Making a Difference (Health Communications, Inc.)

Taste Berries for Teens: Inspirational Short Stories and Encouragement on Life, Love, Friendship and Tough Issues (Health Communications, Inc.)

Taste-Berry Tales: Stories to Lift the Spirit, Fill the Heart and Feed the Soul (Health Communications, Inc.)

A String of Pearls: Inspirational Stories Celebrating the Resiliency of the Human Spirit (Adams Media Corp.)

Gifts of the Heart: Stories That Celebrate Life's Defining Moments (Health Communications, Inc.)

Values from the Heartland: Stories of an American Farmgirl (Health Communications, Inc.)

Stress & Your Child: Helping Kids Cope with the Strains & Pressures of Life (Random House)

You and Self-Esteem: A Book for Young People—Grades 5–12 (Jalmar Press)

Safeguarding Your Teenager from the Dragons of Life: A Parent's Guide to the Adolescent Years (Health Communications, Inc.)

How to Develop Self-Esteem in Your Child: 6 Vital Ingredients (Macmillan/ Ballantine)

Self-Esteem for Educators: It's Job Criteria #1 (Jalmar Press)

Keeping Our Children Safe: A Guide to Emotional, Physical, Intellectual and Spiritual Wellness (John Knox/Westminster Press)

Developing Self-Esteem in Your Students: A K–12 Curriculum (Jalmar Press)

Getting Back Together: Repairing the Love in Your Life (Adams Media Corp.)

Is Your Net-Working? A Complete Guide to Building Contacts and Career Visibility (John Wiley)

Managing Your Response to Stress: A Guide for Administrators (Jalmar Press)

Stress Management Skills for Educators (Jalmar Press)

Problem-Solving Skills for Children (Jalmar Press)

Also by Jennifer Leigh Youngs

Taste Berries for Teens #3: Inspirational Stories and Encouragement on Life, Love, Friends and the Face in the Mirror (Health Communications, Inc.)

A Taste-Berry Teen's Guide to Managing the Stress and Pressures of Life (Health Communications, Inc.)

More Taste Berries for Teens: A Second Collection of Inspirational Short Stories and Encouragement on Life, Love, Friendship and Tough Issues (Health Communications, Inc.)

Feeling Great, Looking Hot & Loving Yourself! Health, Fitness and Beauty for Teens (Health Communications, Inc.)

Taste Berries for Teens Journal: My Thoughts on Life, Love and Making a Difference (Health Communications, Inc.)

Taste Berries for Teens: Inspirational Short Stories and Encouragement on Life, Love, Friendship and Tough Issues (Health Communications, Inc.)

Contents

Introduction

Welcome to *A Taste-Berry Teen's Guide to Setting & Achieving Goals!* This book is for teens and is filled with stories, commentary and advice by teens (ages twelve to twenty) who share their ideas and tell of their experiences about the importance of setting and achieving goals. As most teens know, goals spell the difference between wishful thinking and making things happen. As sixteen-year-old Breanna Hillard explained, "Of all my friends, the most 'exciting' are the ones who make things happen—and to do that, you've got to set goals. An example that comes to mind is when, just recently, Creed was coming to town. Everyone at school was like, 'Oh, it's going to be the hottest concert; we've just got to get tickets!' Well, the tickets were very expensive, and the word got around that the concert would be sold out within an hour of tickets going on sale. Let me tell you, I knew straight away which of my friends would be going to the concert—and which ones would be moaning, 'I wish . . .' Those who made being at the Creed concert their goal lost no time in getting permission from their parents, earning the money they needed, buying the tickets and organizing a ride to and from the concert. I've learned that people who decide on something and then set a goal to bring it about are the ones who get what they want. Of all my friends, it's those who are proactive—those who set and achieve goals—who are the most fun to be around. They're very cool."

As Breanna's statement makes clear, setting goals and reaching them means you're likely to be among those who get to enjoy the rewards. No doubt about it, deciding what you want and setting goals to achieve it are the marks of a taste-berry teen. *Taste berry?*

Yes, a taste berry. If you haven't yet had a chance to read any of the books in the *Taste Berries for Teens* series, you're probably asking, "What is a taste berry?" A taste berry is a glorious little fruit that, when eaten, mysteriously convinces the taste buds that all food, even food that is distasteful, is delicious! In our *Taste Berries for Teens* series, we use the term as a metaphor for being the kind of person who makes good things happen. People are taste berries to each other when they are sensitive and aware of all the ways in which we make each others' lives better, bigger— and sweeter. We are all interdependent upon one another for kindness, encouragement, consideration, assistance and support. Has someone cheered you on when you lost hope and almost gave up on pursuing a dream or goal that was important to you? Has someone reached out to help you when you felt overwhelmed or didn't know what to do in a certain situation? If so, that person was your taste berry. On some days we could all use a taste berry—especially when it comes to the importance of being "all that we can be."

We each have the right—and responsibility—to be "all that we can be." Do you feel you are putting your best foot forward? Setting goals is the key to making your life purposeful, worthwhile, and filled with happiness and people who love and support you. Know that you hold the key to shaping the direction of your life. Believe that you have a responsibility to live your life according to those things you value, hold dear and have a yearning to achieve. "To do, to have, to be" is the essence of being alive. Choose it! Whether you're a master goal setter, or just beginning, whether you've set goals in the past and then felt you couldn't follow through, or have no idea where and how to begin to set goals, this book is for you. Consider it your taste berry for setting and achieving goals to sweeten your journey, to turn an ordinary life into a spectacular one! This step-by-step guide will help you:

♥ Discover what your personality, aptitudes and hobbies reveal about what interests you.
♥ Determine if you are dreaming "big enough" for your life.
♥ Identify goals in nine different areas of your life.
♥ Set long- and short-range goals—for today, tomorrow and "the future."
♥ Develop a plan of action to achieve your goals.
♥ Break goals into manageable monthly, weekly and daily "to-do's."
♥ Remove obstacles that stand in the way of achieving your goals.
♥ Resolve to see your goals as "totally you" and ones you want to commit to.
♥ Learn ways to encourage, coach and inspire yourself to reach your goals.

This book is divided into five units, each opening with *A Message from the Authors,* which is our chance to give you a brief overview of what you can expect to find in the chapter, as well as do some teaching of our own. Each chapter thereafter starts with a story from a teen so that you can see what your peers are up to and what they've learned in terms of setting goals. This is followed by our teaching a specific concept or skill, and then by a "Virtual Practice" section, where you get to apply what you've learned—actually identifying, setting and charting out how to reach your goals.

Remember Breanna who identified those of her friends who set and achieved their goals as "proactive" and "fun and very cool"? You, too, can be these things. Even if you start small— such as setting a goal to do well on your test next Friday—the more you set goals and see yourself succeeding, the more you build a storehouse of positive experiences of viewing yourself as being goal-oriented. Setting goals not only helps you accomplish worthwhile things, but it's good for your self-esteem, too. When you accomplish something you set out to achieve, you see your-self as a capable and competent person. Achieving your goals reminds you that you're a winner! Bottom line: You're cool!

And, cool person that you are, we look forward to hearing from you! We'd love to hear about the taste berries in your lives and how you've learned to be taste berries in the lives of others. To that end, we invite your comments on how you found this book helpful and welcome your stories about how you're coping with teen life. We'd love to hear about the incredibly powerful and positive things you are doing and how setting goals helped you achieve those things. We are now working on a new, upcoming edition of our *Taste Berries for Teens* series, so if you have a story or a poem you'd like to submit, please send it to us at:

Taste Berries for Teens
c/o Teen Team
3060 Racetrack View Drive, Ste. #101–103
Del Mar, CA 92014

Remember, you deserve an exciting and rewarding life, but it won't just magically fall from the clouds. So, if you're ready to start thinking about what's important to you, if you're ready to make plans to "make things happen," if you're ready to shape the direction of your life, let's get started!

Taste Berries to You! Bettie and Jennifer Leigh Youngs

Part 1

Do You and Your Friends Talk About Your Goals?

We meet ourselves time and again in a thousand disguises on the path of life.

—Carl Jung

First say to yourself what you would be, and then do what you have to do.

—Epictetus

A person's ability to choose is the essence of freedom. How well he learns the skills involved in the process of choosing determines his power of self-determination, his freedom of choice.

—Paul Woodring

Success is liking yourself, liking what you do and liking how you do it.

—Maya Angelou

It's never too late to be what you might have been.

—George Eliot

1

A Message from the Authors

When was the last time you and your friends talked about the most important goals each of you have? Maybe you answered that question something like this: "Well, just last week my friends and I talked about our plans to ace the semester finals," or "With the prom coming up, we talked about how we could organize enough of our friends to chip in and pay for a limo." Or, maybe upon reading the question you chuckled and said, "Talking about goals is a geeky thing to do, and none of my friends do it!"

Think about it. You and your friends may not sit down to the lunch table and say, "Okay, let's all talk about our goals," but that doesn't mean you don't discuss the things that you'd like or plan to do, whether for the immediate future, like this weekend, or in the distant future, like two years from now. Even a (daily, weekly or monthly) "to-do" list is an indication you have goals.

Maybe you readily talk about your goals, or maybe you don't. Teens who do discuss their goals with each other say they do so because of one or more of the following reasons:

♥ *All* my friends talk about what's important to them.
♥ The more I talk about what I'd like to do, the more I find out,

for sure, what is really important to me, as well as what is not. This clarity helps me make decisions.

♥ Talking about the things I want to do helps me commit to achieving them.

♥ When I talk about my plans with my friends (and parents and teachers, too), I get a lot of information on how to make my dreams even better or bigger. And I often learn how to do things in a better or more efficient way than when I'm left to my own thinking.

♥ Talking about my goals makes me feel important and like a "somebody" with my friends and family.

♥ Talking about my goals makes me feel like my life is going well, like I'm not wasting my time. And I like how I feel about myself when I'm achieving things that are important to me.

As you can see, it's good to talk about your goals. Talking about what's important to you is a first step in discovering and clarifying who you are and what you want out of life. And, as you'll discover when you work through this book, it's the basis of setting goals that are important to you and of formulating a plan of action to achieve your goals. More on this later, but first we would like to comment on the primary reasons teens say they *do not* discuss their goals.

♥ **I'm not sure what I want to do (and don't want to be seen as lacking ambition).** Probably that's a good reason to set goals—at least those that help you explore your interests, hobbies and aptitudes (more on this in chapters 3 to 6). In this book, you'll get a chance to explore who you are and what you want. You'll learn how to devise a plan to uncover, little by little, those things that make you excited about taking more and more control of your life, as well as plan to have a bigger say in shaping the direction of life—both for the days and years ahead. You'll also get a chance to set goals in nine specific areas, a feat that is sure to leave you feeling that you are not without ambition.

♥ **With my friends, it's just not cool to talk about goals.** Some teens may believe it's not "cool" to talk about their goals, but nothing could be further from the truth. It's very cool to be involved in your life and take an active role in shaping the way your days, weeks, months and years unfold. Look around you; you'll find that many teens are actively pursuing their dreams and ambitions—and whether they speak out loud or let their achievements do the talking, teens with goals are not wallflowers!

♥ **I don't want to risk that others might belittle, ridicule or discourage me in meeting my goals.** It's true that someone may—even with good intentions—discourage you from attempting your goals. Maybe this person believes you've set your expectations too high, believing that the goals you want to achieve are too difficult for you, and that you'll fail to meet your goal as a result. And, of course, someone could tell you (perhaps out of jealousy) that your chances of meeting your goals are "ridiculous" or "preposterous"! It could happen, but are you willing to let the opinion of others stop you from meeting your goals? Hopefully, not. By the way, here's a solution to this: Share your goals anyway. It won't be long before you silence the doubts of "naysayers"—as well as develop the confidence in yourself to not get sidetracked by comments that demean, belittle, ridicule and discourage you from tackling your goals.

♥ **I don't want to set myself up for failure: If I said I wanted to accomplish something, and then didn't, I'd look—and feel—bad.** What if you tell everyone your goal is to get on the pep squad, and you try out but don't make the team? Of course, in the hours and days that follow, your having not made the team will be a disappointment to you. That's only natural. And there will be those who feel, as you do, disappointed. And some will feel sad for you, and there just may be a person or two who is pleased that you didn't make the team. But you did something—you "went for it"! Seldom does anyone meet 100 percent of his or her goals in life. But as an old saying goes, "You always miss 100 percent of the shots you don't take!" So go for it! Know that you'll survive and can even thrive during those times you don't succeed. And there is something else you should consider as well: Most people will not fault you for trying to succeed at your goals, even if you don't hit your mark in the end. And for those who do, you have to ask yourself if you are willing to place their opinion ahead of the respect you feel for yourself in making the attempt to succeed in the first place.

♥ **I'm really not all that clear on how to go about setting goals.** Probably this isn't true. If, for example, you say, "I'm going to get all of my homework done this week!"—that's a goal! You don't have to save the rain forest in order to qualify as having a goal. A decision and plan to pass this week's test, or to stop biting your nails, or to develop a better relationship with a family member, all qualify as goals. And here's some more really good news: This book will help you learn a great deal about setting and achieving goals!

So there you have it: Talking about your goals *is* a good thing—and we're hoping that you're in the group that actively discusses your goals! Clarifying the things you'd like to "do, have, be and achieve" is one of the best ways to have a fun, exciting and rewarding life. Everyone needs to look forward to doing purposeful things. If you had no goals whatsoever, you might feel that life was dull, boring, even depressing. But with goals, you get to actively participate in creating the life you want. And that's what growing up is all about: knowing who you are and what you want, and being proactive in shaping the direction you'd like your life to take.

In the following chapter, you'll meet teens who readily discuss their goals—from small ones to grand ones, from seemingly lighthearted ones to serious ones, from lifelong dreams to recent ones. You'll find stories from teens whose goals focus on immediate problems—such as the teen who had the misfortune of having someone sign her name to a "torrid" love letter to someone else's boyfriend—to teens such as J. J. Bailey, who has been working toward his goal for some ten years and will continue to work toward it for years to come. Whether having one goal or many, whether centered on relationships and love, career and school, or hobbies and sports—all have their place in the busy and active lives of today's teens.

The following stories make their diversity and power very clear. As you read each one, you'll discover that whether teens call their goals "baby steps" or "Eiffel Tower plans," they see them as building blocks toward constructing a life that is interesting and fulfilling. So as you read about their ambitions, be thinking about the goals that are most important to you—both now and in the future. Then, throughout the remainder of this book, we'll show you how to map out a plan and set a steady course for reaching your own destination—achieving your own goals that are important to you, and worthy of you!

Taste Berries to You! Bettie and Jennifer Leigh Youngs

2

Teen Talk: "Goals" That Are (Most) Important to Me Right Now

Is That Eddie Murphy Under All That Makeup?

My eyes were glued to the screen—she looked like she was nearly a hundred years old—but she was only in her twenties! Maybe you remember seeing this sort of incredible transformation of a screen character. Take Eddie Murphy, for example. He can play his handsome self in one scene, and in the very next, a very old white lady! Sitting there in the theater and seeing this remarkable change—and knowing it's Eddie Murphy—you still find yourself asking, "Is that really Eddie Murphy?" And it's all done at the hands of a very skilled makeup artist.

I find the art—and magic—of makeup amazing. I'm so intrigued by how someone who is old is suddenly transformed into someone young, and how someone very young can look old (and all the ages in between). It's just amazing to me that someone attractive can play an ugly monster; a young man can appear to be an old woman; a woman can appear to be a man; and a man can look like the most feminine woman. What incredible illusions—and all due, largely, to makeup artistry.

Seeing it all leaves me with this "I have to do that" feeling. And so, it's become a goal: I'd like to be a makeup artist.

I don't have it all worked out as to how I'm going to reach my goal, but I'm working on it. I can only tell you that excitement fills me even when I walk near a makeup counter in a department store, most especially if there's a makeup artist showing someone how to artfully apply makeup.

I guess you could say I've been interested in makeup for a long time. My mother tells me that as a child, I was always into her cosmetics and wanting to put on lipstick, eyeliner, perfume—and everything else! All my friends are always asking me to do their makeup for them when they have a special date, are going to the prom or want to look "very cool." They tell me that I do it so well and always say things like, "Wow—it's beautiful!" or, "It looks so professionally done."

But like I said, I'm just getting things figured out on how to reach my bigger goal. I know that I'm going to start out by going to beauty school and get a cosmetology license. Then I'd like to get some experience working in a great department store with a really classy makeup department. After that, I think I'd like to contact some local television stations and see if I can become the makeup artist for the on-air TV personalities. (I think it would be sooooo coooool to get a job as the makeup artist with a big television star, like be Oprah's makeup person!) After that, I'll see if I can work in local theater. I plan to do all this so that I can have some good experience "under my belt," then I plan to move on to—well, who knows, maybe I'll be a "special-effects makeup artist" on a movie set. It would be so totally cool to work on a movie in the caliber of *Lord of the Rings!* And I just may—hey, you never know!

So those are my plans to date. I know that working in the motion-picture industry is going to mean I'll need good experience as well as some really good contacts in order to get "my foot in the door." So far I don't have any—but I have to start somewhere, and I plan to. So a few years from now, when you're watching the latest and greatest special-effects movie, try to remember not to leave the theater before the final credits roll, because that's where you'll see my name!

Colette Feener, 16

I Need to Find Out Who Wrote a *Torrid* Love Letter to a Guy at School—And Signed My Name!

Have you ever had someone write a letter and sign your name to it? I have, and it was the most embarrassing, humiliating, degrading and upsetting thing I've ever had happen to me. While I'd like to say that the most important goal I'm working toward is to find a cure for cancer or finding a way to bring all world leaders together and get them to agree on ending terrorism so that every human being in the world can live in peace, the truth is, I can't think beyond my immediate circumstance of finding out just exactly who perpetrated their own little act of "terrorism" on me a couple of weeks ago. So right now, my primary goal is for peace of mind for myself.

It all began when I noticed a really cute guy one morning in the student center. I'd seen him around a couple of times, but didn't know him. He was two years older than I, and because of the way our school is organized, our paths just didn't cross all that often. Until that one morning, when I was hanging out with my friends in the student center and getting juice from the snack dispenser. Standing right near the machine, he looked at me and in a really sweet voice said, "Hi." I took it to mean he was interested in me. I (discreetly) asked around and discovered that his name was Matt Raymond.

For the next couple of weeks, I made a point of going to the student center around the same time—hoping to see him. I didn't see him every morning, but when I did, the same sort of thing happened—his eyes would light up and he'd say hello or wave. I was thinking that it wouldn't be long before we had a chance to talk, and that our relationship would change from eyeing each other to getting to know one another. At my school, it's not cool for a girl to call a guy or make the first move, so I decided to wait things out; I was sure our getting together was just a matter of time.

Then one morning I found a piece of paper with a telephone number and Matt's name written on it taped to my locker. I was positively thrilled and took this to be an invitation to call him. I assumed he'd gone through the trouble of asking around for my name, and that he probably couldn't get my phone number, otherwise he obviously would have called me by now. And of course, he'd also found out my locker number, so I knew he had to be serious about our hooking up. I also assumed that he was too shy to talk to me in the student center with the entire student body watching, and too shy just to meet up with me alone. So the moment I got this "Go" note, I met up with some of my girlfriends and went to the student lounge. Sure enough, Matt was there with some of his friends. Again when he saw me, he smiled sweetly and mouthed "Hi!" I couldn't wait for the school day to be over so I could go home and call him!

"Hi," I said, when he answered the phone. "This is Heather. Heather Cowles."

"I got your letter," he said in return.

"My letter?" I asked and then informed him, "I didn't write you a letter."

"Yes, you did," he said, sounding sort of irritated. "I have it right here." And then he proceeded to read me the most torrid love letter I could ever imagine being written. When he'd finished reading the letter, he said, "It's got your signature on it. In fact, it's signed, 'Passionately Yours, Heather Cowles.'"

"No, really," I said in self-defense, "I didn't write it."

"Well, no need to lie about it," Matt said, not sounding like he was at all sweet, nor like he had smiling eyes. Then he added, "Besides, even more proof of it being yours is that it states you'll call me March 1. Well, in case you hadn't noticed, it's March 1." Now he was sounding not only put out, but sarcastic.

"I called today because I got your phone number today," I said, once again defending myself but feeling really stupid.

"Yeah, sure. Whatever," he replied.

I was stunned and didn't know what else to say. I just wanted to get off the phone and think about it all. Flustered, I blurted, "My mom's wanting to use the phone. I have to go now." Then I hung up.

The next day at school, I purposely avoided going to the student center. I just wasn't ready to see Matt Raymond. I needed time to think about our conversation from the day before and figure out what it all meant. Was he playing a game? Did he have a dark side that had led him to write that letter to get some sort of reaction out of me? But why? It seemed so bizarre. So I decided to just let a couple of days go by and to cope as best I could until I knew what else to do.

Then one day after school, out of the blue, I got a call from a girl I didn't know. She said her name was Terra Reid and that she'd been Matt's girlfriend (to my total surprise!) for five months. Then she started yelling at me, calling me names and accusing me of trying to steal her boyfriend. When I tried to tell her I was doing nothing of the sort, she began reading me the same letter Matt read to me on the phone—the letter I had supposedly written to him. I was so angry, I hung up on her. But she called right back and said she'd come to my house if I didn't hear her out. Then she continued reading the letter. When she had finished it, she threatened that she and her friends would "beat me up" if I didn't stop writing, calling or seeing Matt. She ended her tirade by slamming down the phone.

I was so upset! And even more confused. I mean, how could I be trying to break up her and Matt? I didn't even know she existed! So then I called Matt—which took me nearly twenty tries, because his phone was busy. Finally, when I did reach him, he yelled, "Stop calling me! My caller ID shows you've been calling me for nearly an hour!" So then I asked if he would please just listen to my explanation of what happened, but he didn't want to hear it. He totally yelled at me, like everything was my fault! "Why'd you have to call her?" he yelled. "I didn't!" I said. "She called me!"

"Oh sure," he accused, "like you didn't write me that letter! You are such a liar!"

Well, having heard these words, I was so upset that I couldn't stay on the phone any longer. I cried and cried. What a mess! And worst of all, I have no idea who taped his phone number to my locker, and no idea who wrote him the letter and signed my name to it. I know that none of my good friends would do that, and aside from my best friend, I don't know who could have known that I had a crush on Matt.

I've tried to call Matt yet again to ask him about things, but he's had his phone number changed, and there's no way to find out the new number. And now, whenever I see him, he totally ignores me. I feel like the scourge of the Earth!

So my main goal—aside from my usual one of doing well in school—is to find out who played such a cruel and sinister trick on me. Ferreting out who could and would do this is a priority—and I do intend to find out. I can't understand why anyone would do this to anyone—especially me. I thought I was a well-liked person who was seen as being nice. I want to know who would want to sabotage me like this. Knowing there is an enemy—a "terrorist"—lurking out there somewhere is disturbing, and I want to know who it is. I especially hope it's not a friend or someone within my circle of friends, but I know that could be the case. So now I've become suspicious of anyone looking at me or trying to get close.

Besides being upset, I can't stop thinking about the whole thing. I'm not sleeping well, I'm not eating well, and I get upset easily and cry at the drop of a hat—I'm just not the normal me. I'm thinking of getting the school counselor involved because I'm beginning to feel I need help working through this. So like I said, this whole thing has just consumed me, and until it's resolved, I'm afraid that noble goals such as working to find a cure for cancer or bringing world leaders together to end terrorism are on hold. I've got to find out who committed this "dastardly deed" and why. Today, it is my main goal in life. Hopefully, accomplishing this will be a huge contribution toward not only my peace of mind, but maybe even world peace!

Heather Cowles, 17

Call Me "Dr. Santos"

When I was seven years old, I was hospitalized for spinal meningitis. While I was there, the head doctor on my treatment team, Dr. Hazelton, not only saved my life, but also was really kind to me. Every day, he took the time to make me smile and was always exceptionally friendly. He never treated me like I was too young to understand what it meant to have spinal meningitis and what he planned to do to treat it. He also didn't think I was too young to have an opinion about my treatment. That made me feel very special and as the doctor liked to say, "an important part of the treatment team." I really believe all of this was important to my getting well.

It certainly was a big factor in my goal to become a doctor when I got better and finished school. I knew I wanted to be the same sort of doctor—knowledgeable, friendly and respectful of his patients. Then for a long time, I forgot all about it, until I was in high school and it was time to decide what classes I needed to take in order to get into a college program. This forced me to think about what I was going to do with my life. I knew I wanted to help people. And in remembering the doctor who healed me, I decided practicing medicine would be a wonderful way to use my life. So I renewed my desire to be a doctor.

I believe it's good to visualize myself doing what I hope for most in life, so now I picture myself in a white coat with a stethoscope hanging around my neck, my diploma on the wall, and being able to help and heal others. Remembering my doctor and his kindness, as well as how he healed me by being a great physician, gives me a perfect role model for moving toward my goal. My excitement for being a doctor is at an all-time high.

Being a doctor and healing others are what I hope for most in life. It's what sets the mark I aim for in my grades, and what guides me in the classes I choose. When I go out for sports, I ask myself if I can do so without it getting in the way of my studies—which will take me to my goal to be a doctor. I even turned down a job at the video store because I'd have to commit to too many hours. Instead, I took a job with fewer hours in the hospital cafeteria. Besides, being in that setting keeps me focused on becoming a doctor—which is the goal that I'm striving for most.

Craig Santos, 18
Excerpted from More Taste Berries for Teens

"Stop Gnawing on Those Fingernails!"

I have been biting my nails for as long as I can remember. Until two years ago, it didn't really bother me, although it made my mother furious. She's been trying to get me to stop since I've been a little kid. Nothing she tried worked, and believe me, she tried a lot of things, from wiping my fingers with rubbing alcohol (which has a really nasty taste!) to gloves taped to my wrists (which are very difficult to chew off or pull off, given that your hands are out of commission). Like I said, none of her tactics were successful in getting me to stop gnawing on my nails.

Then, when I entered ninth grade, I noticed that many of the girls had really pretty nails, and I decided it was time to have nice-looking nails, too. So I decided I'd stop biting my nails. Well, breaking the habit of biting your nails is not an easy one— as anyone who bites his or her nails will tell you. That year, I tried a million things to stop. I dipped my fingers in all sorts of bitter concoctions, from hot sauces to offensive gels manufactured for this very purpose. I've bandaged my fingertips, and I've even glued on false nails, hoping that chewing on hard plastic would be a turn-off. No luck! Like my mother's attempts to get me to stop biting my nails, my methods met with very little success as well.

Until a month ago. Under the most embarrassing of situations, I found the motivation to stop biting my nails.

If your school is anything like mine, there are about four "levels" of popular kids. There are the brainy types—always respected at our school, but the thing is, you have to practically be a genius to be "one of the crowd," so it's easier just to admire this group and think they're cool. The second group is the athletes, which, let's face it, is yet another type of genius—body agility. I'm all feet and couldn't and wouldn't trek around the track thirty laps, or be seen running through town, for anything.

So, like the brainy types, those of us who are not gifted with muscles who insist on going for a jog around the world every day, well, we just admire and think this group is cool, too. Then, there are the nerds—and who wants to be a nerd? The fourth group is the social elite, those who have a way to make the rest of us just feel, well, socially inept—but wishing we weren't. I long to be in this group—specifically, I've wanted to be noticed (and invited to hang out) by Janelle Rosen, considered the most cool girl in the class, and Rochelle Watson, considered the most popular girl in the school. Janelle and Rochelle were always nice enough, but never really "noticed" me, if you know what I mean. Then, a few weeks ago at an all-school talent show, I ended up sitting right beside them, and all that changed! Can you believe the luck?

Our school's talent show is a really cool event, and like everyone else, I was looking forward to it. So that I'd look cool that day, I'd borrowed my sister's red sweater, since "color charts" indicate I'm a "winter" and red is supposed to be a really good color for me (which I think must be true because every time I wear red, I get nice compliments). I even had my sister help with my hair. She's eighteen and has learned a lot about how to blow-dry hair so it looks awesome. So I looked great, if I do say so myself—well, all except for my nails. As usual, I'd bitten them as far down as you can imagine, so I hadn't even bothered putting polish on them—I mean, it's practically a waste of time, and sometimes when I do polish them, it seems to me that it only makes the fact that they are barely there even more obvious. Oh, well, I'd just keep them in my pockets.

So here I was at the talent show, sitting right beside Miss Cool and Miss Popular, thinking things couldn't get any better. I mean, everyone *always* noticed Janelle and Rochelle; even being seen with them elevated your "must be cool, too" status.

At our school's talent show, the drama teacher, who is always "host," chooses two judges from the faculty, two from student council and two students in the audience. "Who wants to judge?" Mr. Fitzhugh shouted as the student filming the talent show scanned the room and then zoomed in on a face every few seconds, and projected the person on the big screen on the stage of the auditorium. Well, there were about a billion kids with their hands in the air cheering and begging to be chosen as the judge. The whole auditorium was filled with this air of excitement—and you could only imagine mine, sitting here in the row with Miss Cool and Miss Popular. I watched every move Janelle and Rochelle made, hoping to catch their eyes and flash them a friendly smile. Then suddenly, all got quiet for like an instant, and then everyone started laughing, hooting and howling. I looked around and everyone's eyes were glued to the screen in the front of the room. I stopped looking at the crowd and turned to look at the screen up front. There, larger than life on the huge monitor at the top of the stage, was my image, gnawing on my nails like a deranged and starving rodent who had finally run across a morsel of food. This, in front of the entire school! Worse, I was practically sitting in the laps of Janelle and Rochelle. I was mortified! Even more so when the drama teacher said, "Well then, stop gnawing on those nails, Ms. Kelly, and come on up here." I got out of my seat and made my way to the front of the auditorium, my face as red as my sweater.

So I am determined to work on my goal: I am absolutely, positively going to stop biting my nails—starting this very moment!

Kelly Harris, 15

My Wild, Wild Imagination . . .

As a kid, I had a really, really wild imagination. My mind created one fascinating world after another, and each time, expanded on a previous adventure, the plot thickening. The world of the calculating Professor Canard and his debonair arch-nemesis—The Martini Penguin—was my most favorite "mental playground." With the help of Professor Canard, I traveled throughout the world, foiling the latest diabolical plot of The Martini Penguin. The adventures of Professor Canard ranged from the "Maltese Penguin" to "The Susceptibles" (take-offs on the movies *Maltese Falcon* and *The Untouchables*).

By the time I got to be a teen, the world of Professor Canard was replaced by flashy video games and electronic wonders. Though they dazzled my senses, they never compared to the rich imaginary world I'd created as a kid. Being a mere shadow of the indomitable, imaginative giant of my youth, they couldn't replace my world with its former glory. Luckily, things are changing. Two years ago I took an extension college course in computer animation. The course taught how to three-dimensionally animate anything. Using the tools learned in the class, I began to experiment with creating different worlds. But then I remembered my childhood creation of Professor Canard. I began to model basic shapes and slowly transform them into the characters I imagined. The joy of seeing dreams made reality is incredible!

When I was a child, my vivid imagination provided all the "invisible visibles," but now, I want to see my world in real time, played out exactly how I imagine it. To do this I have to find innovative and exciting tools to assist my mind in reinstating Professor Canard—which is just one of my many goals. I've tried working with clay as my tool toward this goal, but it just wasn't right for me. When working with clay, it's quite unnerving to watch your creation collapse into a pile of mush. Another frustrating quandary with clay is the kiln. Finally, you have shaped a beautiful clay pot that has your heart and soul in it, but a tiny air bubble within the clay causes your creation to literally explode within the fiery inferno of the kiln. In 3-D animation, this can never happen. Physics are turned off when working with "digital clay," and there is no risk of explosion. I believe the appeal of computer animation comes from the ability to work, uninhibited by physics, in a world of your own design.

So what began as my wild imagination has turned into my greatest ambition, and that is to be able to turn this hobby into a career of work in 3-D animation. It's something that attracts and holds me like nothing else. Using my imagination to bring a world with self-contained characters and life into being is positively thrilling. So, by combining two things I enjoy most—computers and art—I'm going to create a career in animation for myself. Little did I know that what I used to amuse me and escape the monotony of general boredom as a kid, would become the "brainchild" behind my goals today—goals that are no longer beyond my wildest imagination!

Thomas Hatfield, 16

"Royce's *Little* Sister"? Oh, Please!

Sometimes I think I'm having a nervous breakdown, but it's only an identity crisis. So it probably comes as no surprise that my biggest goal is have an identity—my *own* identity.

I am in ninth grade, and my brother Royce is a senior. He's cool and has a lot of friends. All the teachers like him. None of this interfered with my life until this school year. Now that I'm attending school on the same campus as he does, I seem to have lost my identity. When I was in junior high, everything was fine: I felt like a real person, an individual with a personality of my own. But now, suddenly, I seem to be reduced to being seen only as a "sister"—"Royce's sister." It's a real drag. The other day I raised my hand in class with an answer to a question, and after answering it correctly, the teacher remarked, "Oh, you're as smart as your brother!" In PE class I was told, "Athleticism must run in your family." Plus, Royce is a regular comedian, always witty and sees the humor in any situation. So everyone keeps expecting me to be funny, too—which I'm not. But who knows, I might be funny if I weren't under such pressure to be. But it was no laughing matter in the cafeteria when I ran into Mike Larson, a guy I have a huge crush on. Naturally when I saw him, I smiled and he smiled back at me. Then the friend with him teased him, saying, "Oh, got a thing for Royce's little sister, huh?" I cringed, knowing that being seen as someone's "little sister" is the kiss of death as far as romance goes.

Royce this and Royce that! It's been more than a couple of months now, and it's gone on long enough! His going to this school and being so well-known affects every area of my life. So, my goal this year is to be seen as a personality in my own right, to be Marissa Farintini and not "Royce's sister." My plan is to look different and act different. For starters, I'm going to put a fuchsia rinse in my hair. It's a very cool look, and the polar opposite of Royce's "preppy" looks. Hopefully—even though it may sound like a baby step—this will help set me apart and stamp me with a personality of my own. Because quite frankly, I just do not want to be identified as "Royce's little sister" anymore. So having my own identity is a goal I intend to achieve—and the sooner, the better!

Marissa Farintini, 14

I'm in the Process of Recording a CD

My biggest goal in the next few months is to complete the CD I'm recording.

To sing professionally has always been a dream of mine, one I've held since I was a very young child. I know precisely when this goal was born: When singing in a choir for a special performance, the stage curtains opened, the lights came up, and I stepped out from the choir to sing a solo in a performance! It was thrilling! Since that day, doing anything other than performing has never entered my mind. It's been the sole driving force behind everything I do—which is a lot! I have been practicing nearly four hours each day, as well as "honing my craft" by doing free local concerts at malls, and singing for birthday parties, at school affairs or for various groups (including senior citizen homes) whenever I'm asked. I leave no opportunity unanswered!

While I'm always busy and it's a lot of work doing what I do, I find great pleasure in singing and never consider it work. Not only does singing give me personal satisfaction, but it helps me cope with the stress and pressures of everyday life. I find that if I've had a really stressful day at school, or if I'm disappointed in myself over something—like getting a bad grade—then when I get home, if I take out my music and sing a couple of songs, my mood changes entirely. You can't be singing an inspirational piece, listening to the melody of your own voice and stay upset or stressed for long. Music is an incredible outlet—or at least it is for me. And to be able to make my life's work around it is going to be just incredible!

I got a voice coach a couple of years ago, something I'm really excited about because, with her help, I've developed my talent way more than I ever imagined. My voice coach, Ms. Amanda Nelson, is someone who believes in me and has encouraged me to never give up my dream of being a recording artist—nor to lose sight of my goal to one day write my own music.

I'm determined to meet my goal of completing my CD—I won't let anything melt my dream to become a recording artist. I'd say that having those goals keeps me motivated to do well in school—which is important because getting good grades is something I have to work really hard at. But I know it's important to graduate from high school and go to college. I know how competitive the world of singing and songwriting can be, so if it takes me years of trying, I want to make a living doing something with music while I continue to work on my dream. I figure that if I have a degree in music, I could use it to teach music either in a public or private school, or even start my own business, maybe doing something like being a voice coach like Ms. Nelson. So, I'm pretty happy with my plan. I feel like I have Plan A and a Plan B. Plan A is the ultimate destination, and Plan B is for until I get there—although I'm definitely going for Plan A! So I hope one day you'll buy my CD, and if you catch me in concert, be sure to let me know you've read my story here. Maybe I'll dedicate the next number I sing to you!

Justina Jasper, 16

Deleting (His) E-Mail

It's been three months since Cole and I broke up. I'm having a really hard time getting over him. The CD mix he gave me remains in my Discman. All of his e-mails are saved in my in box. His varsity soccer sweater is still in my locker. I'm stuck in the moment and just don't want to let go. I know I have to. It's just so hard.

Of all the wonderful memories I have of him, the e-mails are among the most important to me. I just feel that if I were to delete them, I'd be trashing six months of irreplaceable memories with him. It would mean Cole and I were "no more," and that's more than I can handle right now.

Why not move on? I mean, he's not the only guy out there, right? After mentally going down the check list of reasons, I always come back to the same inescapable fact: No one else would be Cole.

I know you're probably thinking, "C'mon, girl! Get over it! Move on." Hey, I say the same thing to myself, but then, I've known Cole! He was perfect! He was the flower-bringing, late-night-phone-calling, insist-on-holding-the-door-open-for-you, kind and considerate guy. He was a perfect guy and a perfect boyfriend. And for six glorious months, he was mine. Even he knew I held his heart in the palm of my hand. He'd go to any length to do special things—like the time I went to camp and he drove five hours to be there on visitor's day! I told him he didn't have to do that, but he said, "Seeing your smile was worth every mile!" You see, I told you he knew how to make a girl feel special.

He begged me not to cry when we broke up, saying it was the hardest thing he ever had to do. Of course, I cried anyway, hurling angry protests at him in between tears. He let me carry on until I had no more words—or tears. Then he told me his reasons for "needing" to leave. He explained that he cared about me, but that eventually we'd have to break up, so better now than later, since it would get harder as time wore on. His "excuse" made absolutely no sense to me at all.

I guess I am getting a little better. At first the mere mention of his name could send me into heart-wrenching sobs. Next came feelings of resentment—not for him, but for the unknown girl who would be next to have his heart.

It's been three months, and I still want him back. But I know it will never be. He's moved on. He doesn't phone, write or e-mail me any longer. So letting go of my memories—and all the physical things that are reminders of him—is the goal I've set.

"Move on . . . get over it . . . get on with your life" are such cool and easy expressions, but so difficult to do. I know I'll never utter them to anyone in my entire life. Still, they are precisely what I must do. Easy to say—but so difficult to do.

I think I'll start with deleting the e-mail. Maybe if I delete one message a day . . .

Lauren E. Anderson, 16

This "Future" Goal Is Not What I'd Intended

I have a big goal, but because of a "complication," unfortunately, it's become a "future goal." It's a complicated story, one that revolves around my love for the game of basketball.

This past year, our school basketball team lost our best players for a simple enough reason: They graduated and are now off to college. Of course, this meant there were any number of positions open—well, actually, there was a whole new team to build. I really wanted to be on the team and was sure I would be.

Being on the team is not just a matter of showing up. At my school, you have to try out and get selected for the team. This is cool because, once you're named as a player, everyone knows you've earned a spot on the team, so there's a lot of respect that goes along with being an athlete on any team at my school. Also, practically everyone knows how good playing a sport (especially on a winning team) looks on your college transcripts. So all in all, there are a lot of benefits to playing a sport. And I was ready to start the perks coming my way.

So the new season of practice and eventually tryouts were at hand. My goal was to get on the basketball team—end of story. Practice sessions started, and I attended every one of them. I arrived early, played all the way through and didn't leave until well after practice ended. At least that's the way I started out. For some reason, I began to slack off a little—not only in playing my heart out on the basketball court, but also in not putting my heart into my studies. Needless to say, my grades slipped.

This alarmed my coach, because at our school, keeping our grades up is an important criteria for being on a team. The coach scheduled a meeting with me and also had the assistant coach attend. He told me he was concerned that maybe I wouldn't be able to handle varsity-level playing, and he felt it best if I discussed with my parents whether I should play basketball or simply focus on my studies. He said to let him know what my parents had said the following morning. I vowed right then and there that I'd "fix" the problem—but for some reason, I didn't say these words out loud, so of course, the coach really had no way of knowing I darn well intended to kick into high gear. Not speaking of my commitment was my first mistake, but not my last.

I went home that night and talked things over with my mom. But I never discussed things with my father—which was another of my seemingly many mistakes. I went to practice the next day, but since I hadn't looked the coach up that next morning to tell him what my parents and I had decided, he hadn't been expecting me to show up at practice. When he saw me, he said he needed to talk with my father. He called him, and my father came to school immediately. I was told to wait in the car while they met. So there I was, sitting in the car waiting, as my dad and my coach talked over my ability to handle the lengthy basketball practice and the game competitions, while still having time for my studies.

When my father returned to the car, he said the coach had told him he was disappointed that I hadn't discussed the situation with him the prior evening, and that maybe I just wasn't taking things seriously. Therefore, it was probably best if I wasn't on the team! I was so upset and disappointed—and I knew that I brought a lot of their decision on myself.

That night my parents and I had a long talk. I told them I was going to change, and I promised to do better. Knowing how much I wanted to play, they said I should try once more to meet with the coach and try to convince him I was capable of handling both being on the basketball team and keeping up my studies. Well, I spent my entire lunch period trying to convince my coach. But he was resolute, adding that even should he give me a period of time to see if I could successfully handle keeping up with both, if I couldn't, he'd find it hard to ask me to leave the team.

Devastated, that night I told my mother of the conversation I'd had with my coach. She said I should give it "one more try"! So again I went to the coach and told him that if he gave me a chance and then decided that I still couldn't handle it, he could kick me off the team and I wouldn't complain. He told me that he would think about it and tell me the next day. But the next day his answer remained the same: He didn't feel it would work out. And that was that! I was not on the team!

Well, you can probably see how I learned a few lessons through all of this—so I won't go through each of them! All I will tell you is that my goal to be on the basketball team is stronger than ever. You can be sure I will do everything I need to in order to reach that goal next year—no halfhearted playing; no half-hearted studying. I'm starting now. I shoot hoops with my friends every chance I get. And though I didn't make the team, I never miss a game, because not only is it important for me to study moves, it's also important for me to keep up my team spirit. What's more, I've never studied harder. I know that keeping up my grades will come easier to me if I never let them slip and take this time to build some really strong study habits. So my future goal definitely takes work today, but I know that next year you can look for me on the basketball court because I'm putting the work in today to make sure that's where you'll find me!

Kimberly Holcombe, 15

I'm J. J. Bailey—Remember the Name!

My name is J. J. Bailey. It's a name I hope to make famous—which is a goal I've been on for some time.

For as long as I can remember, I've played soccer. I just love the game. I watch it on television, and whenever I get a chance, even attend the local college games. So when my friend's grandfather, Mick Guy, invited me to go with him to a University of San Diego (USD) men's game, I jumped at the invitation. Being there that day, I found my life's goal!

Sitting there watching the game, I was struck with how incredibly skilled each team member was and by their intensity—which I could even feel sitting way up in the stands. The home team was playing a really great team, so they were pretty equally matched. So there they were, tied and now into overtime. Suddenly, a player cracked a shot from the top of the box—it was such a thing of beauty—and the goalie had no chance! It was a shot that won the game. Feeling his joy and the power of the moment, the player pulled off his jersey to reveal a T-shirt underneath that read "Beat UCLA." Jazzed, he ran up to the stands and jumped up onto the railing, where he was hoisted up by screaming fans who mobbed him in a whirlwind of congratulations. It was so cool!

I knew right there that I wanted to play soccer—and play for USD. So that was the goal. But I knew it wasn't going to be easy. You see, I'd always been a decent player, even standing out at times, but I never had that something extra it takes for people to really notice me. But then I got lucky and found a team that was very good. So that improved my skills, plus the coach worked with me so I improved even more. I was starting to get looked at by professional talent scouts, and I was having more fun than ever playing ball. Then during my third year playing for this team, my junior year in high school, I dislocated my hip and tore a ligament in my knee. I was out for a while. The worst part was the timing, because the State Cup was only a month away. It looked as if I was going to have to sit out during what could conceivably be the biggest tournament of my life. I was bummed!

Well, I did have to sit out, and the team found another defender to take my spot—someone who was a better player than me. This is where it goes from bad to worse. My coach was stepping down, and a new coach would be taking over for the next year. I was in a bad spot. I had to impress some guy who had maybe seen me play once or twice, and I had to convince him that I was capable of playing at this level. Well, that wasn't going to be easy, because I hadn't run or touched a ball except once before tryouts, since I'd been hurt only four weeks prior. Needless to say, I didn't make the team.

I can't explain how something like that affects you. This team was my family; I loved the guys and, more than that, I loved playing with them. But now they were something from my past. For a while I was just bitter and felt like giving up, but then a few months later, the new coach called me up and asked if I would play in a tournament with them because a few of their players had picked up injuries. I said yes immediately. I just wanted to play ball again.

As it turned out, I had one of the best tournaments of my life. Better yet, the coach told me that if it was at all possible, he would put me on the roster for good—but that never happened. But he did inspire me to work at my goal again. So I worked out by myself for a while, and then one day, the coach of my old team called me up and said I could practice with his new team. I jumped at the chance.

Now, because of my hard work, I'm closer to where I need to be to make the team at USD. In fact, they have sent a scout to watch me play.

So, I'm on my way! Like I said, J. J. Bailey's my name! When you see it in the headlines on the sports page, you can say, "Oh, good for him! He made it!" Because I intend to.

J. J. Bailey, 17

The Smoothie Decision

When I was born, my birth mother put me up for adoption. Then, when I was eleven days old, a couple with one child of their own adopted me. I was told that my birth mother was only fourteen years old when she had me, but other than that, I know nothing else about her. Now, nearly fifteen years later, my birth mother has "located me" and wants me back in her life. I just found out a couple of months ago. I was surprised about this, of course, and I have to admit I was feeling really good that she cares enough about me to do this, even though I didn't have any idea what her being in my life would mean. I already have two parents—a mother and a father—and I love them very much. Still, I have always yearned to know and meet my birth mother.

When my parents first told me that my birth mother (a term I find strange, but easy to use) wanted us to have a relationship, I knew that while in the beginning it might be a little awkward, it could be a good thing, too. So I was all for this big change in my life—as long as spending time with her didn't mean that I'd have to change schools, or give up my friends or my parents. I told my mom and dad that I was nervous about meeting with her, but excited, too. That's when things started to get complicated.

I quickly learned that's not the way my adoptive parents feel. Even though they told me my birth mother had contacted them and wanted to see me, they hadn't planned on my feeling okay about meeting her. I could tell they were disappointed that I would even consider seeing my birth mother—and they were even more shocked when I told them I'd like to have a relationship with her. Now they're against my even meeting her, as are some of my other relatives. They're telling me that my mom and dad don't deserve to be hurt by having me spend time with my biological mother. Then they point out how "unfair" my seeing her would be to my "real family."

I know they're being protective, and I think they might even be a little frightened that I might leave the family and go off and start a new life with my "real" mother. I've thought about their fears. And I also think about my birth mother's fears of never seeing her child again, ever. Even though she "gave me up," I'd like to think that there must have been some very compelling reasons as to why she made that decision. I mean, she was only fourteen when she had me, and I'd like to think that she thought it was best if adults cared for me and raised me and gave me a life that she probably couldn't. So I truly understand why she put me up for adoption and can even see how it was for the best. Even though it hurts to know that I was "given up," I've forgiven her for it.

One day several weeks ago, my (adoptive) mom told me that she didn't think it was a good idea that I see my "biological mother" until I was older, because she'd read that it creates so many complications that most children are more likely to be harmed than to benefit from it. When I told her I wouldn't allow that to happen, and that I was convinced that I wanted to meet my birth mother, she took me to get a smoothie. While we sat at the smoothie shop, she pleaded with me to wait to see my birth mother until I was eighteen. And then she admitted she was afraid she would lose me and couldn't bear it.

I was so stunned, and scared, too. My parents (and aunts and uncles and cousins and sister) were all I had ever known. They were all I had. There was no way I would ever give them up. My mom and I cried and hugged, and I knew I had to wait to see my birth mother. Sitting there with our smoothies, I made the decision not to have a relationship with my biological mother until I reached the age of eighteen.

So that's how things are right now. For now, I have to live with the choice I made—and there really is no other choice. Still, an important goal in my life is to meet up with my birth mother on the very day I turn eighteen. There are a lot of things I have to do to make that happen. Unfortunately, I don't know how to find my birth mother because my parents won't tell me her address or, for that matter, anything about her (although they said they would tell me when I was eighteen). So I'm secretly going about trying to find her so that when I do turn eighteen a couple of years from now, I'll know where to find her.

I hate harboring this secret, but I know how much it would hurt my mom if she knew I was looking for my birth mother now (before I was eighteen). I'm hoping that when I do get to meet my birth mother, my parents will see that having a relationship with her doesn't mean I won't ever stop loving them; nor will I stop considering them as my mother and father.

So meeting my birth mother is a huge goal in my life, especially now that I know she is reaching out to me. So while I'm going about my life, getting good grades so I can get into a good college and working on being one of the best players on my school's tennis team, the most important overall goal in my life is reconnecting with my birth mother. I just wish it weren't as complicated as it is. But like I said, for now, it's the way things are.

Regina Deanne Lewis, 16

The Liver Report

My goal has always been to be liked by the really popular crowd. But that was before I met Haily, a girl in my health class—someone I really didn't know too well. Our teacher assigned a report on the liver and paired us students together to work on the report. I wasn't too thrilled about the assignment or the academic "buddy system." I thought doing a report on the liver couldn't be all that much fun, and doing it with someone I didn't even know had to make it even more of a chore.

But the next day when class time arrived and the teacher told us to get together with our "partner" to begin working on our reports, Haily and I pulled our desks together and began to work. We started out by drawing a giant picture of the liver on tag board, and then went through the textbook to do some research on the liver. By the end of class on the second day, we'd completed our assignment. Like a couple of other students in the class, Haily and I finished early. Someone asked the teacher what we should do next, and she told us partners to just sit together and talk quietly. I did not want to talk to Haily. I didn't know her, and just because we'd spent two class periods doing a report didn't mean she was my new best friend. So, I just sort of sat there, looking around the room.

"Our report is boring," Haily said, breaking the silence. "It needs something else."

"Like what?" I asked, thinking she was only trying to start up a conversation—and was obviously unaware that I wasn't interested in talking.

"It needs something funny," she replied, her face all animated. "Let's ask the teacher if we can interview some of the teachers around school on what they know about their liver and report back to the class what they said."

"We could, but that wouldn't be funny because they probably

know enough about it," I said, thinking it was a really stupid idea.

"You're right," she acknowledged, and then said, "So let's take my parents' video camera, go to the mall and go up to people and ask them what they know about their liver. While they're answering, we'll roll the camera. I'll bet we get some interesting and funny responses from 'street strangers.'"

"That's a good idea," I admitted, and then realized I'd just agreed to her plan. So that weekend we took her video camera to the mall and interviewed people. It was fun. Really fun. I acted the part of a reporter while Haily was the camera "crew." Just like Haily predicted, it was interesting and we got some really funny responses. Some of the people we interviewed knew next to nothing about the function of the liver, and we even ran across one person who didn't know where her liver was located, because when we asked, she said she thought it was "somewhere in the chest region"! One person even said that people who drink alcohol often have to have their liver cut out, and someone else said it was "related to the lungs." Still another person said it was called "liver" because it was the only organ you couldn't live without. (He looked baffled when I asked him about the heart or brain and said he didn't think they counted as organs!) All and all, Haily and I had a lot of fun.

Our working together that day was the beginning of our friendship. Somewhere during the three hours Haily and I spent interviewing "street strangers," I discovered that although she was different from all my other friends, she was someone I'd like to be my friend. She is very outgoing, full of ideas and is someone who doesn't back down from a dare. Shortly after our liver report project, she and I were standing in the student center and Bubba Watts came over and dared her to down a bottle of Mountain Dew in one minute. Without blinking an eye, Haily accepted his dare and guzzled down the soda in forty-five seconds flat!

So now Haily is a part of my circle of friends. I'm enjoying that she's a different personality from me. For instance, I really appreciate her sense of humor and how she's able to turn even an ordinary assignment into something fun. And she does that with everything; she just always sees the humor in a situation. And she's gutsier than I am, always "pushing the envelope," so to speak. She's ready and willing to take on a challenge, or go the extra mile; she does whatever it takes to do something better. I really like that about her.

I'm so glad she taught me to go the extra lengths needed when it comes to having friends. So I'm thinking that my goal of being "really liked by the popular crowd" is not really what I mean. It's more like "really being a good friend." The change is a big one: I've decided to be more open-minded when it comes to making friends, and to look at how another person's differences can be a plus. So that's a goal for me: to keep an open mind when it comes to people, and to not be so judgmental. Being judgmental can be limiting, and I don't want to limit myself in that way. I guess you just never know how a new friend might be brought your way—she could even come via a liver report!

Sarah Erdmann, 15

To Swim with the Dolphins . . .

Even as a young child, I was captivated by the way dolphins glided gracefully, effortlessly, through the water. Watching them always felt like magic! So much so that when I was ten, I asked my mom if we could call Sea World in San Diego, California, to see if there were any jobs open for someone as young as me. I thought maybe I could be an assistant trainer. We called, but of course, we were told that Sea World was not quite ready to hire someone without a degree in biological science, nor a background (or experience) working at the world-famous theme park. Though immensely disappointed, I knew my lack of qualifications ruled me out: All I'd ever done was visit aquariums. Well, that, and I had written a few reports on dolphins. But alas, it wasn't enough. Although Sea World wasn't ready to put me on the payroll, they did offer a summer camp for kids interested in working with marine life. You can only imagine my excitement! Ta-dah! Dolphins, here I come!

Going to the camp was so exciting, I could hardly sleep at night anticipating the next day. Interacting with the animals was what I cherished most. Like a bear attracted to honey, for the next three summers I attended Sea World camp. Nothing mattered more to me than summer coming and getting to attend Sea World camp—where practically everyone knew me on a first-name basis. But things were about to get even better!

The summer of my fifteenth birthday, I got to fly to Sea World in Florida and actually swim with dolphins. I spent ten whole days learning in-depth how to train and work with animal behavior. Not only did I discover the joy and magnificence of learning about the bottlenose dolphin, but I also got to experience firsthand their magnificent power when I rode on their backs and played with the most astonishing of animals. This most amazing experience crystallized, for me, that the only way

I can be truly happy in life is to reach my goal of being a dolphin trainer, where I will get to experience my lifelong desire to swim with and work with these magnificent creatures. I sure hope that you'll get a chance to take a swim with one, but if you don't maybe you'll have the opportunity to see me as I do. Because I know the day is coming when audiences all over the world will cheer as I soar through the water on a dolphin's back. My goal is set, and I'm already on my way toward making it real!

Buck Plevyak, 15

To Wear Makeup,
Own Cool Clothes . . . and Be a Writer

My Aunt Carla is sooooo cool! As a youngster, I remember watching her every move: how she walked, how she dressed, how she wore her makeup, the color of her nails, the hint of perfume, the way she laughed. I remember thinking, *I just have to be like her! She's beautiful and so "with-it." She's got the world's coolest friends, she's smart, and she is so popular, her phone never stops ringing.*

Whenever my family would visit her family, I'd sneak into her room just to be there and see the way she kept her things. I'd open her closet and, if I felt I could get away with it, slip on her pair of cool white boots. I'd go to her dresser and look at all her makeup—she had tons of it—and sometimes I'd snap on her clip-on earrings. I'd even lie across her bed, imagining that her room was mine—and that I was her—because certainly I wanted to be. She was my idol.

Once when I was visiting her, she invited me to her room and read me a story she had written about our grandfather. I was impressed, of course, but amazed, too, because getting a story published was completely foreign to me, and it seemed like the most awesome thing anyone could do. Because I really liked my grandfather, I couldn't hear the story enough. I asked my Aunt Carla time and time again to read me the story, and she always did.

Of course, the story was special because it was about my grandfather, but it was special for another reason, as well: My Aunt Carla had written it and had it published in a book. I knew for sure that I wanted to write a "real" story and have it published in a book (not just in a magazine), and vowed that one day I would. So I got busy writing—or at least that was my intention. I got out paper and pen, but no words came. I told my Aunt

Carla that writing must be a really tough thing to do because I'd tried, but was having no luck. "You have to be inspired," she informed me. Still, no inspiration came my way. I didn't give up easily: Over the next few months I wrote a few things, but nothing held my attention—until my baby cousin, Ciara, was born.

Like everyone in the family, I'd been looking forward to her birth. But when I learned that this beautiful newborn had been born deaf, I was really upset, thinking how awfully unfair that was. Here was a tiny little girl who couldn't hear. Never would she hear her mother's voice—or anyone's for that matter. Never would she hear the birds sing, nor the singing of any hot new band—she wouldn't even hear lullabies. And though I had just purchased a new lullaby book with nursery rhymes set to music, and had been so looking forward to giving them to her, she wouldn't be hearing a word or note of it. I felt so sorry for her; it was sad that a little child would never be able to experience the world of sound. I felt frustrated, and I was angry, too. Going to the computer, I opened a page and wrote and wrote and wrote. Like a million emotions tumbling over and over each other, the words flowed. Rereading my words the next day, I realized I'd written a passionate—and inspired—"real" story. I gave it the title, *Ciara's Music Box*.

Right about the same time, I was reading *Taste Berries for Teens*, a book of stories for teens by teens, and because the authors invite teen readers to submit stories of their own, I mailed my story right off. Shortly thereafter, I learned that my story was accepted and was going to be published in their newest book, *A Taste-Berry Teen's Guide to Managing the Stress and Pressures of Life*. The book came out this past year, and so, like my Aunt Carla, I, too, am a published author! And, of course, I've reached my goal of writing a story and having it published.

My Aunt Carla was really impressed. She told me that she knew I was creative, and that I should continue writing. I thought about that, but wondered—and doubted—if I would ever be able to "outdo" my first published story. Certainly, I was inspired by Ciara's circumstance—but it was so unusual. Would I have to wait for incredibly profound things to happen before I was inspired to write, and if so, what if nothing really inspirational happened? I voiced my concerns and frustrations to Aunt Carla. This time she told me that a writer doesn't just wait for inspiration to come to her, but rather, that it's her mind that produces the inspiration—and it does this because "a good writer always fuels her mind." She explained this was done by observing people and "life" closely, and by "reading, reading, and reading." So that's what I'm working on developing now. I'm really motivated to do well in my English classes, and I no longer skip over electives such as literature or creative writing. Now, I consider courses such as these vital to developing good skills as a writer, and, of course, as powerful ways to "fuel" my mind. So I realize I'm in a new phase in my goal. Whereas I once wanted to be a "published" writer, now I want even more. My goal is to develop my skills so that I can be a *good writer*, and so that I can continue to get published.

I'm thankful that my Aunt Carla turned me on to this; I so admire her. I still look to her for guidance and encouragement when I need someone to be supportive. But with my newfound confidence, these days I've been telling her that if she ever needs advice on writing, to just call me up—especially now that I'm about to be published for the second time in a year!

Mandy Martinez, 16

"Extra" Weight

"Does it hurt to be big?" a little girl once asked me, her large baby-blue eyes looking up and down my size-eighteen body. Totally surprised at the question, and knowing she was too young to understand exactly how offensive such a question was, I answered softly, "No." If I'd been honest, I would have answered, "Yes! It's a totally devastating experience—but only when the emotionally illiterate among my classmates make fun of my weight." But what would a little girl do with a response like that?

Even knowing her question was asked in innocence, it bothered me because I took it to mean that my "extra" weight must be a painful look, even to one as young as she. For sure, some people in my school think it's a painful look, judging by their subtle, yet snide, remarks and a certain glance, a snicker or the really obvious exclusion from a certain circle of friends.

I cope as best as I can, but it's tough. Sometimes I try not to notice the reaction of others, to continue to say and do nothing. But sometimes I feel as though I should just let myself go and say exactly what's on my mind, or better yet, burst into tears, just to show those who taunt and tease me how their comments really affect me. But I know I won't, so I continue to fake a smile and go on pretending I'm a good sport about it all. But I don't think I'm going to be patient much longer. Though it may come as a surprise to some, my biggest goal in life is not to be thin, but rather to get good grades, do well on my college-entrance exams and get accepted into a good college. And yes, I am healthy and know the importance of not being "extra" heavy—but it's my goal, and not anyone else's business. So to my list of goals I've added, "Be *extra* patient, tolerant and kind to my classmates about my weight issue," even though I feel that my having to do that is asking me to pull their "weight," too. Why? Because in order not to have my feelings hurt by their remarks—words that only serve to make me feel indifferent, or worse, unattractive—I'm the one who has to make concessions—and compromises. So to anyone reading this, pull some "extra" weight yourself: Be tolerant.

I don't mean to belabor the point, but if you're someone who ridicules others because of their weight—or for any reason—I suggest that you treat others the way you want to be treated. It's a simple enough idea—there's nothing complicated about it. If you wouldn't want to be teased or embarrassed, don't tease or embarrass someone else. If you wouldn't want someone to call you names or point out your shortcomings, don't call them names or point out their shortcomings. If you want people to be kind and respectful of you, then be kind and respectful of them. It's a most important goal—and one everyone should aim to accomplish. I'm pulling my weight by adding this "extra" goal to the top of my list of goals—I hope you'll pull yours by adding it to the top of your list, too.

Shire Feingold, 15

Religiously Looking . . .

I've always been curious about how (or if) God would find his way into my life. Our family doesn't go to church, and while my parents taught me right from wrong, they never use the word God or refer to any religious rules to teach me those things. Nor have they ever said that it was important to have what my good friend Melannie calls a "personal relationship with God." I've asked my parents what religion we are, and they say we don't have one, although my mom said her family used to go to an Evangelical Lutheran church once in awhile when she was growing up.

So most of what I know about religion comes from my friends, but I'd have to admit that talking with them raises more questions than answers. I have friends who are Catholic and Protestant. One of my friends and his parents are Native American, and they go to a sweat lodge and sacred dances. Another one of my friends is Jewish, and he and his family go to temple every Saturday. Yet another one of my friends is Muslim and worships at a mosque. I even have a friend whose family is from Vietnam, and they are practicing Buddhists. Having friends who believe in different religions makes me wonder how many religions there are in the first place, and then I wonder how they are alike and how they differ from each other. Last month I was with two of my friends, Josh Levine and Sean Sandersohm, who got to talking about the "Golden Rule." (Sean called it a "spiritual principle." I had no idea it was a spiritual principle—I mean, I thought it was just a wise and practical "old saying.") Josh was saying that he could think of at least six religions that believe in the Golden Rule, and when Sean challenged him to name them, Josh did. I learned that the Golden Rule (the "do unto others as you want them to do unto you") principle is shared by Buddhists, Jews, Muslims, Hindus, Christians and Confucians.

Well, it was all news to me. So now that I've learned that many religions share the same ideals, I really wonder whether or not some religions are "better" or more "right" than others, and is there one that is "best"?

So I'm really curious, and I want to know more. I know that some faiths even have a different "sacred" text, or scriptures. For example, I know from talking with my friends that for Christians it's the Bible; for Jews, it's the Torah; and for Muslims, it's the Koran. My friend Singh, whose faith is Hinduism, says the sacred text for his faith is the Veda. But other than these "bits" of knowledge, I don't have a clue about what these various texts mean for followers in terms of how they should lead their lives. But I want to know more, especially since the September 11 attack on America—when the terrorists justified their acts as following the mandates of their religion—only to have others from the same faith completely deny that the tenets of their faith would sanction terrorizing (and killing) others.

I'd have to say that I'm also curious about the big deal that some make about how people of different faiths are allowed to demonstrate their spiritual beliefs. I mean, once when a classmate volunteered to lead the class in prayer before taking placement tests last year, the teacher told him he couldn't, explaining that prayer was forbidden in schools. But then, after the terrorist attack on September 11, I heard everyone from the president of the United States to school leaders say how important it was that we all turn to prayer to find comfort and understanding. People everywhere were praying openly for the victims of the terrorists and for our nation—on radio and on television, even in the Senate. Calling on our faith was suddenly okay, and in fact, important. "God Bless America" was everywhere, on billboards, on people's lips as they sang it and said like a prayer across the nation. People were talking about spiritual things like the need to be kind to each other.

So, on the one hand, it feels good to know that I'm not alone in my search for understanding, but on the other, I'm definitely starting out at "ground zero." So you might say that I'm religiously looking for a religion, a faith that I can call my own. It's a very real and important goal in my life. Because, eventually, I do want God to find his way into my life.

Brad Rogers, 17

Your "Yo-Yo" No More!

No guy wants to be treated like a "yo-yo," and I just broke up with my girlfriend because of it.

Shannon and I went steady for two years—if you can call what we had "steady." She was always breaking up with me and, in my mind, for no good reason. I can understand, "My parents are upset that my grades are so low and say that it's because I'm spending too much time with you"; or "I want to date someone else." But Shannon wouldn't give me a reason. We'd break up, and then she'd come back and say breaking up was a mistake, so she'd want to get back together. We'd have a great time for a couple of weeks, and then she'd break up with me again. Throughout it all, I was expected to tolerate her on-again/off-again feelings for me.

She even expected me to follow certain rules for our time apart. During the time we were "broken up," we weren't supposed to speak to each other in the cafeteria at lunch, or leave notes in each other's locker, nor was I allowed to walk her to class. Calling her at night would be grounds for a huge argument. This game would go on for a week or so, then, out of the blue, she'd decide we should get back together, and the opposite rules would then apply. We'd be back together for a month or so, until she broke up with me again, and the game would repeat itself. It was so exhausting, and not very much fun.

Finally, I said "no more." It was really sad to break up, but I just couldn't take the ups and downs and back-and-forth games anymore, nor the way I felt about myself for being with someone who treated me in this way and totally disregarded my feelings.

At first, Shannon acted like it was no big deal, that I'd be back when she got around to having me back. When I didn't play her game, she got upset. She said she couldn't understand how I could refuse to take her back—especially because (as she reminded me) I had once told her that I loved her. I told her that love isn't supposed to be so one-sided, and that going with someone is supposed to make you feel good, not uncertain, and not as insecure as I felt with her. But it's tough not to take her back. I really do have feelings for her, and it's not like I'm interested in anyone else.

But I definitely want to stop feeling—and acting—like a yo-yo, so no matter how much I'm tempted to take her back, my goal is to not to. I plan to be around people who help me feel good about myself. So as far as relationships are concerned, my goal is to find a girl who honestly appreciates being with a nice, easygoing sort of guy. One thing is for sure: My next girlfriend will know it's important to treat me like I'm more than just a toy—a "yo-yo" she can take down from the shelf and bat around, then put back after her games. Setting this goal has helped me with my even bigger goal of learning to feel better and more confident about myself. It seems to me that when you feel good about yourself, all goals are easier to reach.

Curt Davidson, 17

I'm Getting Married—
In a Matter of Weeks!

I just got engaged! My fiancé, Danny, is a year older than me, and in his first year of college. We plan to get married next year on Valentine's Day. I've got three months of high school left, and when I'm out, I plan to get a full-time job and plan our wedding. Because I'm so excited about it, I tell everyone we're getting married in a matter of weeks—which right now means in about fifty-eight weeks!

We'd both like to have a really beautiful wedding with a lot of guests; I've already bought some bridal magazines to get some ideas on dresses and how to plan a perfect wedding. It's a very happy time for us. We went together for three years in high school, and even though we're young, we feel we're mature enough to make a go of things. We talk a lot about the life we'd like to have, and our plans for making all our dreams—and now our goals—come true. We talk about everything from the "dream home" we'd like to own one day, to the children we'd like to have. Both Danny and I grew up as only children, so we know we don't want just one child! We both agree that growing up without brothers or sisters is a lonely experience (at least that's how the two of us felt growing up).

The other day my fiancé and I were looking through one of the bridal catalogs together. When we came to a page where there was an adorable flower girl and ring bearer, Danny joked, "Do you think we could order one of each of those?"

His question brought to mind something I used to believe in childhood. When I was little, I used to think you could buy children from a catalog. I can distinctly remember being a very young child and seeing a mail-order catalog with kids in it and thinking the children were for sale along with the clothes. So I worried that if I wasn't "good," my parents might "buy" a child from the catalog, and send me away for some other family to buy—as if there was some "Kids-for-Less" catalog!

Of course, I now know that you can't just "buy a child" (from a catalog of all places), and I've long figured out that it's unlikely my parents would ever send me away. I think that the family life I had may have a connection to my goal of wanting to be married and start a family now, as opposed to going off to college and having a career and postponing marriage and family. When you've seen how good it can be, it's easy to want to re-create it for yourself. It's really important to me to have a family that is very close-knit and loving.

Even though I grew up in a very loving home, I know how terrible it is when that's not the case. I think of friends I know whose parents have divorced and then one parent moves far away, leaving the children without two parents that they can see on a daily basis. That was really hard for them, and I wouldn't want my children to have to go through something like that. I also had a friend who ended up being placed in foster care, and it was a very tough experience for him. He lived with his mother, who had a serious alcohol problem, and I guess he never met his dad, so that affected his life, too. It was awful.

I have a close relationship with my mother and father, and I can't imagine not being with them while growing up. I'm completely dedicated to being the kind of mother and wife it takes to have a great family. It's my greatest goal in life, so when Danny made the remark about having "one of each of those," I smiled and assured him, "Well, if ours don't behave, we'll go ahead and order those!"

Tammie Harmon, 18

Shutting Out Jackson-Brown

When I was twelve, my parents got me a puppy, a Pom-Poo (part Pomeranian and part poodle). I named him Jackson-Brown because my last name is Brown, and my dad loves the music of Jackson Brown, so I've listened to his music at home all my life. While I liked the music, I loved my puppy Jackson-Brown. And it was easy to tell that he loved me. He slept in my room at the end of my bed. Jackson-Brown would moan softly when I left for school in the morning or for a soccer game on the weekend, and he'd be right there by the door to greet me when I got home. It was so sweet! He'd be so happy to see me that he'd turn around and around, sometimes getting himself so excited that he would pee on himself (and on the floor)! That part wasn't so sweet, since I had to clean up after him. But I loved him anyway. He was great—just a little dog that wanted to be with me in everything I did. I'm sure he thought of us as a twosome. He liked my parents all right, but he loved me.

Last year I started making more friends, and they would come over to my house after school. I'm sure Jackson-Brown decided that if these were friends of mine, they'd be friends of his, too. When my friends came over, Jackson-Brown would run in, thrilled that "he and I" had company and jump all over everything. Sometimes my friends and I would have clothes laid out on the bed (or CDs or homework) and he'd be dancing all over them. And if we had any food, of course, he'd want to eat it. So I always had to chase him out and shut the door to my room so he wouldn't interrupt us. I'm sure he felt abandoned, and he'd give me a really pathetic "sad eyes" look. I'm sure that he thought it would work; it often did. But sometimes, I just wanted to be alone with my friends, especially if a "new" friend came over and I wanted to get to know her—and have her think I was cool. I mean, not everyone likes other people's pets. And, of course, with Jackson-Brown, he thought he was the attraction! No self-esteem problems there!

One night I had four girls come to my house for an overnight stay. We were playing CDs and baking pizzas in the kitchen. You can only imagine how happy and excited Jackson-Brown was with all this commotion. In fact, he was irritating me, and I just wasn't in the mood to deal with him. I opened the door and commanded him to go outside. He looked at me with those sad eyes, as though apologizing. With his head lowered to the floor, as if saying, "I'm sorry and sad," he sulked out the door. Then I shut Jackson-Brown outside of the house so he wouldn't get in our way.

Though he had never left our front yard before, Jackson-Brown decided to leave the yard this night. About an hour after my forcing him out of the house, I began to feel kind of guilty and went to let him back in, but he wasn't there on the porch like I expected him to be—nor was he anywhere in the yard. "Jackson!" I called, and then whistled for him, but he didn't come running. I called and called for him, and still he didn't come. Starting to panic, I got my parents and friends to help me, and we set out with flashlights, all of us calling his name and looking for him, but he was nowhere to be found. Finally, my dad called off the search and said, "It's time for you girls to go to bed. We'll try again in the morning." My mom said, "Maybe he'll come home by himself before then."

I was so worried, I could hardly sleep that night; all I could think about was my dog and how much he loved to jump up on my bed to be with be, especially if he could sense that I was feeling stressed out over something, like an argument with a friend. He always knew how to read me. If I was mumbling over a having to take a big test, he'd jump around all happy, begging me to take him for a walk. He was just so sensitive—what a great dog. And the thing with my friends—well, he just wanted to be part of the fun. I just wished I'd had more patience with the poor little thing.

I don't know when I finally fell asleep that night, but I'm sure it was almost dawn. Still groggy, I woke up to the sound of scratching at the back door. Suddenly, I realized what I was hearing, and my eyes popped open and I jumped from the bed. I ran to the back door and opened it—but it was just my imagination. There was no Jackson-Brown pouncing and wiggling and wagging his tail, happy to see me.

We still haven't found Jackson-Brown, and it's been two days now. I put up signs, but no one has called. I'm working on a flyer with his picture on it, and I plan to have them ready tomorrow. Finding him is my number-one goal. I've gone door-to-door throughout the neighborhood. I went to the pound yesterday and plan to go again tomorrow. I've called the Humane Society and on the way to school check to make sure the signs are still up. I'm placing an ad in the "Lost and Found" section of the newspaper tomorrow. I'm a girl with a lot of goals, but right now none seem as important as finding my dog.

Jensen Brown, 13

Making Parole . . . in a Few Months

When I was in the seventh grade, I started smoking pot. My mother found out and tried to get help for me, but I didn't want to stop and didn't. With continued drug use, by ninth grade I was really out of control. I was such a problem that I was placed in a center where I was diagnosed with ODD (Oppositional Defiance Disorder). I was put on seven different medications, which did help me control myself, but the moment I got out, I stopped taking my meds.

That was a huge mistake, because once I was off the medications, I felt anxious and stressed out. So I started using again, and used harder and harder drugs. I'm ashamed to admit it, but by the time I was sixteen, I was using cocaine every day. And I was stealing from my family and friends to help support my habit.

Then I got my seventeen-year-old girlfriend pregnant. At four and a half months into the pregnancy, we found out that the baby had several heart problems as well as a severe curve in his spine. Rather than helping her and supporting her through the pregnancy, even knowing our baby was going to be born with health problems, I turned away from her and the baby. I didn't contact her until months later.

Then my own health became a problem. Because I was using drugs and had been for some time, the lining of my nose was being eaten away, and as a result, I couldn't breathe properly. Plus, I was always getting sinus infections. You'd think that would have caused me to stop using, but instead of doing that, I started using in a way I hadn't before: I started using crack.

By the age of eighteen, I was into criminal activities to support my drug habit. Though I didn't get caught in the first few months, eventually I did. The day before my eighteenth birthday, I was arrested and charged with thirty-eight felonies. I was given a lengthy sentence in a correctional facility, and have served eleven months so far. Life in prison is more awful than anyone can describe, though I can tell you, it's a horrible, horrible life. My entire existence is scheduled. I'm told—make that ordered—when to shower, when to eat, where to sit when I eat and, of course, it's not like I have a choice of what's on the menu. But having lost my freedom is not the worst part.

The worst part is knowing that I've crushed my family: Their son, brother—and father—is serving time in prison. My sister graduates this year, and someone will have to videotape it so I can see it—I won't be out by then. My son will be two years old in July. I've only seen him once. I haven't held or kissed him. Ever. I don't want to be the type of father who never sees or holds his son.

I am getting help for myself in turning my life around. I'm getting treatment for the ODD, and because I am, my thinking is more rational; I'm more focused on important things. I want more out of life. I'll be twenty in a few months, and this is not where I want to spend my birthday.

Being incarcerated is a consequence of the criminal acts I committed, which were a consequence of my drug use, which was a consequence of my being just plain stupid and not using my common sense, which was a consequence of my not putting any worthwhile goals in place in my life. I didn't even set expectations for myself. I just lived in the moment—and for me, the moment was always about drugs. But no more.

I'm sorry for all the people I've hurt, and for all the ways I let myself down. I'm really working on it. I'm reading everything I can in hopes of learning a few things. For starters, I'm reading about the importance of a child's early years, and how a child's self-esteem depends upon the way his parents love and care for him. I'm really interested in learning all I can about ways I can better communicate with my son's mother so I can develop a relationship with her that will be good for my son, and for the two of us as parents. And I want to continue my education and go on with that as far as I can. I plan on attending a career exploration program that's offered here at the prison. It starts in a few weeks. And I plan on learning everything I can about ODD so that I can work with my diagnosis and excel in spite of it. I absolutely intend to get out of here as early as I can, which depends on a lot of things—good behavior, for one. Well, you can bet I'm getting mine under control. I want to change my life, my thinking, my behavior—I guess, put simply, my goal is to change.

But I'm certain I am going to achieve it. I can't waste any more time. I'm already behind because of the ways I've messed up. So don't ever use drugs. Even if someone suggests that you just "try it," don't do it. No good can come from using it—and trust me, drugs will take you so far from your goals that you'll be playing catch-up, like I am.

Jason Smith, 19

Do You Believe in Fate?

Do you believe in fate? I'm trying to decide if I do. When I was a very little girl, my dad opened a video store. He hired a guy by the name of Alvin D'Arcy, who ended up working for my dad for a number of years. Sometimes I'd go to the store with my dad, so I got to know Mr. D'Arcy—and his young son, Blane, who would sometimes come to the store to wait around for his dad to get off work. Blane and I had a lot of fun walking around the store, finding our favorite children's videos, and telling each other about the movie (or how many times we had seen it). Then came the sad news that Mr. D'Arcy's father passed away, and he and his family were moving to the same town as his mother so that she wasn't all alone.

Then one day, five years later, when I was in sixth grade, I went to school one morning, took my seat and noticed a new boy in the class. I smiled and said hello to him, and knew right away that he and I would get to be friends. Then the teacher introduced him. When she announced his name, I couldn't believe it! Although I hadn't recognized him (he looked really different than I'd remembered), it was Blane D'Arcy! I was so happy to see him. At recess, we talked and talked! His family had moved back to town—which was good news to me. I liked my friend, and because we had memories of all those times in the video store when we were little, it was like we were secretly extra-special friends.

Then, two years later, my parents moved to another town—a long way away. My father had bought a very big video store, and by now had a business partner. They had plans to acquire other video stores and turn them into one big chain of video outlets. So I knew we'd be living in this new town for a very long time and that probably meant I'd never see Blane again. But I knew I would never forget him, either. Then, several years later, I was visiting a cousin of mine in her town, and she told me about a party being given by one of her friends. So we were at this party, and you're never going to guess what happened! In walks Blane D'Arcy with a couple of his friends! And so it was that our paths crossed yet again. What are the chances of such a thing happening? The moment Blane and I spotted each other it was like, "Oh my gosh, I can't believe it's you!" We were so happy to see each other. So we talked and caught up on all that had gone on over the couple of years we'd not seen or heard from each other. Then I learned something that just blew me away. Blane had been my cousin's roommate for the past year at college! We'd each changed so much, but what hadn't changed was our friendship. Well, that's not entirely true: I can't begin to describe the chemistry between us! It was awesome—so awesome that we agreed to become a couple! So then we talked about how I could enroll in the same college the next year so that we could be together all the time. You can't believe how happy all this makes me!

When I told my girlfriends about Blane and I meeting up and now dating, they said things like, "It was meant to be!" and, "It was in the cards" (even "in the stars"). Another friend said, "It's fate."

All of this has got me to thinking: What is fate? How does fate differ from coincidence, or even synchronicity? One of the first things I learned in my quest for answers and more knowledge on all this was that our chance meetings—again and again and again—may be "synchronicity," which is, I learned, a term coined by Carl Jung and meaning the coincidence of two or more events where something other than the probability of chance is involved. See, now isn't that something that sounds interesting to explore? It is to me.

I've decided that I've been given this incredible set of circumstances in my life, and I plan to find out what it all means, what's behind it. I want to know if "fate" applies to everything and everyone, or just certain incidents and people. Blane and I obviously have something special together, and I'm curious to know more about this whole notion of "fate" and "synchronicity." It's absolutely a goal of mine. I've already gone to the library and checked out books on the subject, and I'm researching Web sites on the Internet, too. I intend to keep studying and searching for answers until I have a clear understanding. Because what we have is too good to leave to chance!

Candee Randol, 17

My Important Goal Right Now

If you'd like to write about a goal that is important to you, do that here. (If you'd like, send it to us for consideration of having it published in our next book!)

_____

_____

_____

_____

_____

_____

_____

_____

_____

_____

_____

_____

_____

_____

_____

_____

_____

_____

Part 2

Who Are You?— Setting Goals That Are "Totally *You*"

What lies behind us and what lies before us are tiny matters compared to what lies within us.
—Ralph Waldo Emerson

When people show you who they are, believe them.
—Maya Angelou

I am not afraid of storms, for I am learning how to sail my ship.
—Louisa May Alcott

It's not just the mountain we conquer, but ourselves.
—Sir Edmund Hillary

If I have lost confidence in myself, I have the universe against me.
—Ralph Waldo Emerson

3

A Message
from the Authors

When you read over the goals and aspirations of the teens in the previous unit, were you surprised to learn that goals could apply to so many areas of life—and in so many different ways? Whether the goal is to change the world, or to deepen your own understanding of yourself, whether to discover or uncover your interests, talents and hobbies, or to make the honor roll, looking and planning ahead—hoping, wishing, wanting, dreaming—are all phases of setting goals for creating the life you wish to have. Today's teens are determined to make their wants, wishes, hopes and dreams come true.

There is a difference, of course, between "wishing, wanting and hoping" and "making your dreams come true." Setting goals is the key. If you are like most teens, there are a million-and-one activities (and distractions) that fill up your time. Having goals is the biggest difference between those teens who accomplish a great deal (or who are on their way to doing so) and those who profess to want to achieve certain things but never seem to make them happen. Achievers focus their time, task by task by task, to accomplish their mission.

Setting goals is the formula for success: Goals point you in the direction of where you should focus your time and energy. By channeling your efforts in a specific direction and on specific tasks or activities, you are more likely to achieve those things you want to accomplish. In short, heading in the direction you wish to go increases your chances of getting there. Best of all, feeling that you're making strides toward accomplishing those things you'd like to "do, have and be" is a good feeling—and an empowering one.

Having a happy and satisfying life—both now and in the future—is largely about doing those things that are interesting and important to you. But first you have to have some idea of what is interesting and important to you—your needs, values and aspirations. We can be unique in what we want—as you no doubt gathered in reading the stories by teens in chapter 2. While one teen may wish to become president of his or her class, another may wish to be the person behind the scenes helping that person get elected president. While one person may choose to focus his or her life solely on raising a family, another may wish to focus time and energy on the care and nurturing of animals. While one person may retreat to the desert to conserve and preserve the natural resources of our environment, another may choose self-expression via the arts or by developing his or her athletic prowess. Your personality, aptitudes and hobbies tell a lot about who you are. In this unit you'll get a chance to see what yours reveal about you, and learn ways to make the most of these personal and precious attributes. Let's examine these things more closely.

Your personality: Some say that our personality is an innate (inborn) part of who we are. As such, our personality isn't something that changes a great deal. For example, if you are a gregarious person, you're outgoing and not shy. Probably you like to be with people and therefore prefer doing activities where others are involved, as opposed to doing tasks all by yourself. "Who you are" information is incredibly important in helping you make decisions about what sort of life and lifestyle you'd like. It is also an important consideration in choosing what career might be right for you, even what "regimen" of activities you're more likely to stay with in meeting your goals to be healthy and stay fit.

Who you are is revealed in the clothes you wear, in those hobbies and activities in which you lose all track of time, and in the types of friends with whom you most enjoy spending your time. As you'll see in this unit, all this is useful information that you can use to set goals to get your life, lifestyle, leisure, work and personal needs met. For example, let's say you're wondering how you can incorporate your personality in choosing a career most feasible for you. If you don't like to be outdoors, it is unlikely you will want to apply to be a firefighter or a conservationist. If you love being outdoors, and if you love nature and working with animals, then you may want to consider work that allows you to do that, and to pass up a job that demands that you be in an office all day, working with facts and figures on the computer. If, on the other hand, you really like working with people, especially helping people work through problems, then you may not want to consider being a veterinarian—unless, of course, you work primarily in the front office, talking and interacting with the pet owners. This unit will help you look at other ways you can set goals that are a part of your identity.

Your aptitudes: Our strengths—the areas in which we learn most easily—are different for each of us. Perhaps you've always had a talent for writing great letters and stories, and it comes easy to find the right words for any report. On the other hand, your best friend has to really work at any written assignment, yet she never forgets anything that is laid out as a picture in front of her, like a map. This is because we each have different aptitudes. In chapter 5, you will learn about nine types of intelligence. But here's the catch: Rarely, if ever, does anyone have a "high" aptitude in more than two or three of these nine areas. The trick, of course, is to find which two or three come naturally—and therefore easily—for you. Here's some great news! In this unit, you'll get a chance to discover which are your best (and yes, your worst) aptitudes, and how to set goals that allow you to promote your strengths.

Your hobbies: Because your hobbies display your talents and natural skills and interests, they're also a great source of information about "who you are." And, because our hobbies allow us to uncover our talents and interests, they bring about joy and satisfaction within us. Guess what? This information can be useful beyond our own inner contentment: While you may think of your hobbies as "just for fun," they can point you in the direction of an exciting job or career goals, and help you set goals to develop friendships with others who share your passions! In chapter 6, you'll get a chance to explore your innate interests and set goals that allow further exploration.

Pretty exciting stuff, don't you think? From understanding your personality to knowing more about your aptitudes and interests, this unit will help you think through who you are and how you can make the most of your assets. Then, later in this book, you'll get a chance to incorporate your newfound knowledge into your goals and your plans for achieving them.

So, who are you? Have you thought about what you want out of life? Do you have a plan for getting it? This unit will help you get more clarity on those answers, which is a terrific step in setting those goals that will help you feel fulfilled, achieved and worthy—which, of course, is what being a taste berry is all about.

Taste Berries to You! Bettie and Jennifer Leigh Youngs

4

Your Personality: Setting Goals That Are in Sync with Your Personality

Robin Williams: "A Pain in the Butt"

In his acceptance speech for winning an Academy Award for his performance in a motion picture, Oscar-winner Robin Williams thanked a number of people, including some high-school teachers. "Some of my teachers thought I was 'a pain in the butt,'" he laughed, referring to himself as a jokester, a funny bone who could always see the humor in things as a teenager. Then, clutching his Oscar and growing serious, one of America's most beloved comics remarked, "but one special teacher said to me, 'I hope you'll channel that talent. You'd make a good public speaker!'"

Excerpted from Taste Berries for Teens Journal

"Who" Are You?

Most people have heard of actor and comedian Robin Williams, a man who has certainly succeeded at tailoring his career to fit his personality. Consider the importance—and joy— of letting your personality shine in all that you do. Of course, you'll need to have a good sense of who you are. Robin Williams probably has a good sense of himself. We'll bet that if he were asked to identify some of his personality traits, probably he would list things like: "I love to be with people; I love to be funny; I love to be outrageous; I love to make people laugh; I love to study people, to see what makes them tick. Stuff like that." No doubt Robin knows all the things that make him Robin Williams.

How fortunate that Robin's teacher encouraged him to recognize his personality traits and to consider them strengths, and coached him to do something with them. It was to be the start of something very special—as many people know. As his Academy Award confirms, the "pain in the butt" found a way to fashion his personality into a very brilliant success!

We're betting that a few years from now, the same will be true for some of the teens you met in chapter 2, such as Thomas Hatfield, whose "wild imagination" is the very personality trait that points him toward his interest (and career goal) in 3-D animation. How about you? What is your personality, and what does it say about you? Here's a chance to take a closer look!

VIRTUAL PRACTICE: UNDERSTANDING YOUR PERSONALITY

What sort of a "personality" are you? In each of the following sets of traits, check the one that best describes you.

❑ I'm quiet and reserved.
❑ I'm talkative and outgoing.

❑ I like to be with a lot of people, even large groups or a crowd.
❑ I prefer to be alone or in small groups.

❑ I'm an "up-front and out there" sort of person.
❑ I'm a "behind the scenes" sort of person.

❑ I'm a high-energy person.
❑ I'm laid-back.

❑ I love animals.
❑ I don't particularly like to be around animals.

❑ I much prefer indoor activities over outdoor activities.
❑ I prefer outdoor activities over indoor activities.

❑ I'm a good listener, sympathetic and compassionate to the needs of others.
❑ I'm not particularly interested in the trials and tribulations of people.

❑ I love working with people.
❑ I prefer reading, writing or working on my computer than working with people.

❑ I'm disciplined and a self-starter.
❑ I'm spontaneous and prefer just going with the flow.

❑ I love being a team player (doing things with others).
❑ I have an entrepreneurial spirit (I prefer to go it alone).

❑ In my spare time, I prefer to hang out in my room.
❑ In my spare time, I prefer to do things with others.

❏ When it comes to my leisure time, I prefer solitary, but physical, activities, such as rearranging the furniture in my room or riding a bicycle.

❏ When it comes to my leisure time, I prefer solitary and quiet activities, such as reading.

❏ When it comes to my leisure time, I prefer to be social and active, such as shooting hoops or playing miniature golf.

❏ When it comes to my leisure time, I prefer social but quiet activities, such as listening to music or going to the movies.

❏ When it comes to sports, I prefer to be a spectator.

❏ When it comes to sports, I prefer playing to watching.

❏ When it comes to clothes and my appearance, I prefer being casual more than being formal.

❏ When it comes to clothes and my appearance, I prefer being formal more than being casual.

❏ I like to write about things.

❏ I like to read about things.

❏ I prefer "doing" more than writing or reading.

❏ I like to be a leader, giving others direction.

❏ I prefer taking directions and carrying out what needs to be done.

❏ I prefer to figure things out on my own.

❏ I like working with my hands, actually creating or repairing things.

❏ I'm an "idea person," who would rather design things in my head and on paper and leave production to someone else.

❏ I'm better with written instructions on how to do things.

❏ Given the choice, I'd prefer to study alone.
❏ Given the choice, I'd prefer to study in a group.

❏ I learn best by hearing.
❏ I learn best by reading.
❏ I learn best when I can see a visual, like a timeline or photos.

❏ In order for me to buy into something, I need facts and proof.
❏ I'm a spiritual person and find it easy to have faith in things; not all things need a concrete reason for being in order to have merit.

❏ I would consider it more fun to read a book about hiking up a mountain than to actually hike up a mountain.
❏ I would consider it more fun to hike up a mountain than to read a book about hiking up a mountain.

❏ I'm the friend who is most comfortable going along with what the group wants to do.
❏ I'm the friend who is making suggestions and decisions and telling the group how things are going to be.

❏ I have a funny bone; I look for the ironies and humor in a situation.
❏ I tend to be a serious person.

❏ I spend my money as soon as I get it.
❏ Saving money comes naturally to me.

❑ I most enjoy spending my money on "things to do" (concerts, dances, movies, horse-riding, going to the zoo).

❑ I most enjoy spending my money on "things to have" (clothes, CDs, hair products).

❑ I most enjoy spending my money on "ways to be" (I'm naturally interested in self-improvement, such as being a better communicator, learning a second language, toning my body, sharpening my intuition).

❑ I prefer to "seize the day" and live in the moment.

❑ I prefer to "think about tomorrow" and plan for the future.

❑ When spending time with friends, I'm usually the one doing the most talking.

❑ When spending time with friends, I'm usually the one doing the most listening.

❑ When I hang out with friends, I prefer going to the movies or a concert.

❑ When I hang out with friends, I prefer sitting around sharing the latest news and ideas we each have.

❑ I prefer hanging around with just a few close friends than being in a large group of friends.

❑ I prefer hanging around with a big circle of friends as opposed to being with just a couple of friends.

❑ I'd prefer to be alone in my room or play with my pet than spend time with others.

❑ What people think of me is important to me.

❑ I'm not as concerned about what other people think of me, as long as I'm comfortable with myself.

Write down any other statements that you feel describe your personality.

♥ _____

♥ _____

♥ _____

♥ _____

In looking over your responses to the exercise you've just read, what trends do you see? For example, is it apparent that you prefer working in groups rather than spending time alone (or was the opposite true)? Do you prefer "machines" to people—or was the opposite true? Do you prefer spending time with animals more than time with people—or was the opposite true?

Make a list of the trends that emerge from the profile above. For example: *I'm social, like people, prefer group activities, like to be active, prefer being the group leader.*

I am a person who: _____

_____

_____

_____

_____

_____

_____

_____

_____

_____

Our personality is fairly evident to those around us. Ask the following five individuals to give you three words that best describe you. Write down what they said.

♥ _____, my favorite teacher, said he/she would describe me as a person who _____

_____

_____

♥ My father (or stepfather) said he would describe me as a person who _____

_____

_____

♥ My mother (or stepmother) said she would describe me as a person who_____

_____

_____

♥ _____, my best friend, said he/she would describe me as a person who _____

_____

_____

♥ _____ (name of friend/coach/or other) said he/she would describe me as a person who _____

_____

_____

Now look back over the statements of those you've asked to describe you. Do you see any "trends"? For example, do their comments or description of you suggest that you're a "people-person," or a "behind-the-scenes organizer"? Do they describe you as "outgoing," "shy," or as a "private person"? Make a list of their comments, grouping together those that seem a lot alike.

Understanding the traits that make you into the person you are is more than interesting information. Knowing your personality can help you set goals that are in sync with your identity. For example:

Fitness: "As a PE elective, should I take tennis or volleyball?"

Social: "Should I try out for the pep squad or take a photography course?"

Learning: "Should I sign up for one-on-one tutoring, or join a tutoring group?"

If you know that you enjoy group interaction more than solitary experiences, then naturally you'd sign up for being in activities where you'd be with others. And, of course, if your personality preference is more of enjoying self, introspective or one-on-one experiences, then you would naturally choose activities accordingly.

Knowing your personality can also help you make choices about jobs or careers in which you feel you're best suited. Asking (and answering) questions such as, "Am I an 'up-front and out-there' sort of person, or a 'private, behind-the-scenes' sort of person?" can then help you make choices such as: "Would I enjoy being a comedian?" or, "Do I have what it takes to be a private detective?" "Should I plan for working with animals?" or "Am I a 'mechanics and machines' sort of person?" Or, "Do I need to be around other people in order to be most happy, creative and productive?" "In choosing the 'setting' for my work, would I prefer a job that allows me to be mostly outdoors or indoors?" "Would I prefer a job where I constantly travel to new places and am always meeting 'new faces,' or would something like that not suit me at all?" "Would I like to work for myself, and if so, would I prefer to work from a home office where it's just me and my office, or work alone but in an office located in a busy downtown high-rise?" Of course, lifestyle and job and career choices are something you'll get a chance to discover more about when you take courses such as career exploration. But if your goal is to make, as Jennifer Youngs says, "Your joys your jobs; your toys your tools," then knowing about your personality is important and useful information.

What other ways can you think of to use the information you've discovered about your personality to shape goals for your life, now and in the future?

_____

_____

_____

_____

_____

_____

_____

_____

_____

_____

Where can you go, or whom can you turn to, to learn more about and to explore your personality on a deeper, more formal level? For example:

♥ *I could check with my school counselor.*

♥ *I could take a weekend course at a junior college near me.*

List them here. (If you have no idea, be sure to list who you could ask who would know your options for finding out this information.)

♥ _____

♥ _____

♥ _____

♥ _____

♥ _____

It's Up to You!

You can use the new insights you've gained to direct you as you set goals for your life. But personality is just one indicator of "who" you are; "aptitude" is another. Like our personality, our aptitudes reveal what comes easily (naturally) for us—and what doesn't. In the following chapter, you'll learn about the seven very different aptitudes, and which ones are a "natural" for you, as well as which are not! You'll also get a chance to see how you can use what you learn to shape goals for creating the life you want.

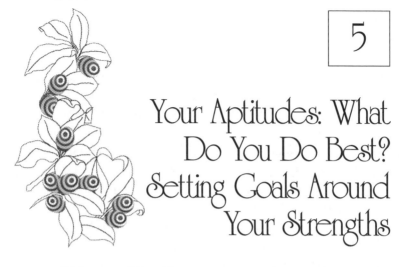

5

Your Aptitudes: What Do You Do Best? Setting Goals Around Your Strengths

When I Finally Knew—"For Sure"

It was only the two of us, my friend and me, standing on the stage of a huge auditorium, every seat in the house taken. All eyes were on us. And though I was the one making the speech—and my best friend was there "just because"—she was so nervous that she said she felt she was going to vomit. I, on the other hand, was enjoying this moment and found it nothing short of thrilling and exhilarating.

My being there just felt so natural. I guess it all began when I was a freshman and took a child-development class at school. As part of our class work, we had to complete a certain number of hours doing volunteer work with children. I chose the day-care center down the block from our school, assisting the day-care teachers with the children's class assignments, as well as play-yard duty. I really enjoyed it, but then, I've always been the sort of person who enjoyed babysitting children. I thought it was a lot of fun. I find kids interesting—you never know what they might say or do—and they're just so cute!

One day, the teacher talked about some of the work she used to do at Casa de Ampara, a center for abused, neglected and abandoned children. I couldn't help but think of how difficult it must be for children to be away from their parents, their home, their toys—I mean, probably there is relief, but it has to be difficult, too. I felt so sad for those children—even though I knew it was in their best interests to be taken care of and to have a safe place to live. So when our teacher expanded our assignment and asked us to get involved in community service—in a place where we hadn't already served—right away I knew I wanted to volunteer at Casa de Ampara.

As it turned out, completing my volunteer hours was an incredible experience. I was alarmed to see that such young children can be faced with such tragic circumstances like abuse and abandonment. So I knew my time there had to be meaningful and make a difference to the kids. Sometimes when I arrived at Casa and asked for my assignment for the day, they'd say, "Read to the kids," and sometimes it was "Play with the kids." Playing with the children, helping them to have fun, to laugh and learn games brought them such happiness. Doing this with other kids as well (you'd be surprised how many little kids don't know how to share their things with others, or even how to be kind to each other) is important to their social development. My time at Casa was a precious experience for me.

It was also insightful. I found out a lot about how the "child protective system" works; I also found out about other programs that help children who find themselves facing the harrowing experience of being in a foster home for years and years, with the courts too overloaded to do anything about it. One of those programs was Voices for Children. This nonprofit organization (with thousands of volunteers) helps children (who have been stuck in the court system for years) become eligible for adoption.

Though I'd met my quota for volunteer hours in my class, I stayed on as a volunteer for Voices for Children. I really just helped with mailing lists and office tasks, but it was a great experience because it taught me even more about programs that help kids and about the special help that so many children need. You should see the files and files of kids who are "backed up" in the court system. It's really appalling. There are literally thousands upon thousands of children who are "wards" of the courts.

Then, on September 11, 2001 America was attacked, and the World Trade Center was destroyed. When I learned that thousands had perished in this horrific terrorist attack, my first thoughts were about all the children in day-care centers in New York City whose parents wouldn't be coming to get them that day. Inside, I just hurt for them, and I wanted to do something to help. But what? I couldn't go to them, since I was on the other side of the country, but I could find a way to raise money to send to them. But how? Who would I get to help? Then I remembered that in a few weeks there would be a community meeting scheduled in the school auditorium. All the area business owners would be there, and a huge community picnic would take place. That took care of the when and where! As for who would help me, the most likely candidates seemed to be my friends; maybe it could be a project for my civics class and the kids in my church youth group, too. Finally, I needed to figure out the how. It had to be minimal cost, maximum profit. I couldn't get clear on the one perfect thing—was it a product or a service?

For the next few days, my "cause" was all I could think about. As I drove to school, I noticed all the flags and patriotic signs that had gone up all over town. They were on the freeway overpasses, in front of houses and businesses, even on our school's scoreboards and bulletin boards. An idea began to formulate, and by the time I pitched my fund-raising goal to my civics class, I was able to suggest, "We can sell something patriotic—something red, white and blue."

"Like pins or flags?" someone asked. "How about ribbons?"

"We need to keep the costs down," I told them, and it all took off from there. We took up a collection at school and within our communities and collected enough money to buy red, white and blue ribbons and some nice stickpins. Then I put together a production committee, and we made these simple looped red, white and blue pins—five hundred of them—at barely pennies each. I got together an advertising committee with some of the best artists and computer graphic masters on our school campus. We created flyers and got out the word of our cause and where we'd be fund-raising on the day of the picnic.

Everything seemed to unfold perfectly. I'd set up shifts to cover our booth at the picnic. Our set-up committee, public-relations committee and clean-up committee all performed their jobs like clockwork. We set up a table outside the auditorium so that everyone coming into the auditorium to attend the presentation would first have to pass by our "Ribbons for the Children" sales table. When the event was over, especially after my on-stage pitch, we were sold out. We made over nine hundred dollars, since a whole lot of people donated even more than the one dollar we were asking. The money was sent to the Red Cross, earmarked for the children who had lost parents that fateful day.

After the event was over, I was struck by how much I had enjoyed—and had been energized by—it all. I especially relished being on stage and making the presentation to such a large group. I realized that I had always been most happy when I was organizing things and leading the way to make them happen. While I lean toward events that focus on making the lives of children better, it's the organization of the cause that is most enjoyable for me. So many people have remarked that I have a "knack" for organizing and working with others—and now I believe it.

I guess that was the moment a real career and life goal took shape for me—that's when I really knew for sure what I'd like to do with my "natural ability." I thrive on organizing others toward a goal. I find it easy to do. This has made me think that I'd like to get a degree in something that would help me get a job with an organization such as the United Way, or even fund-raising—something that allows me to make the lives of kids better. So that's where I'm at right now, finding out what degree would best help me do what I'd like to do. I'm also looking into organizations, such as the United Way, and trying to find out more about what they do. And I've already asked Sandra Osborn, senior fund-raiser for Casa de Ampara, if I can spend "Shadow Day"—where you get to spend a day with a professional in the community—with her (she said yes!). So that's what I'm up to now.

Sara Knorr, 18

What Are Your "Strong Points"?
What Do You Know "for Sure"?

Sara Knorr has a special knack for organizing others in meeting a common goal, especially when tied with her great interest in helping children. She put two and two together and realized that this was special and important to her, and that she could make things happen. Along the way, Sara also discovered what she wants to do for a career.

Finding those things for which you have a natural curiosity and attraction is important information in letting your natural abilities shine. Have you had a particular experience, like Sara, that made you realize you had a certain passion for what it was you were doing or involved in?

Our strengths—the areas in which we learn most easily—are different for most of us. Perhaps your friend has a talent for picking up the latest dance steps within moments of being shown, while you have to really work at it and, even then, find yourself talking your way through the latest move. Another friend seems to have a real talent for remembering things she sees but is not so good at remembering things she hears. Perhaps you, like Thomas Hatfield in chapter 2, have a natural ability to work with the computer, even finding the idea of creating 3-D animation to be a snap, while your best friend is still fearful to use a computer for fear she'll touch a key that will "crash the hard drive and everything on the computer will be lost." What accounts for such disproportionate differences in our abilities? It's because we each have different aptitudes. Harvard psychologist Howard Gardner has discovered at least nine different and distinct types of intelligence. His research suggests that we are "good" at only a few of these—which means that we are not so good (and in varying degrees) at the others.

This is useful information. Not only does it confirm why some things are easy for us while others are more difficult, but such information can steer us in the direction of setting and achieving goals accordingly. So what are your strengths? Of the nine aptitudes, which ones come easily for you, and which are the most difficult for you to master?

The following exercise can help you find out.

VIRTUAL PRACTICE: DISCOVERING YOUR "STRENGTHS"

Read all nine types of intelligence, and then go back and decide which is your strongest point, then the second best, and then your third and so on, all the way through to the ones at which you are simply not so good. Use 1 to indicate your strongest area, the type of intelligence that is easiest for you, all the way to nine being the least easy for you.

_____ **Verbal or Linguistic Intelligence.** This is your ability to read and write, to use words well. Writers, speakers and politicians develop this type of intelligence. People who are linguistically intelligent are systematic, enjoying patterns and order, which is why they enjoy word games and have a good memory for trivia. This is the teen who gets voted in as a class officer, writes for the school paper, turns in terrific term papers and remembers jokes—even those knock-knock jokes from elementary years!

_____ **Logical or Mathematical Intelligence.** This is your ability to reason or calculate. People who have well-developed logical intelligence like to count and be precise, such as scientists, mathematicians and lawyers. They are good at deductive thinking, using computers and problem-solving, and like the orderly basis of programming and application. This is the teen who enjoys his math classes, keeps his room and closet fairly organized, and will remember that your borrowing his CD time is up!

_____ **Musical or Rhythmic Intelligence.** We often classify musical ability as a "gift," when in fact it is an aptitude, an intelligence. Musically intelligent people are very sensitive to the emotional power of music and find it easy to learn dates and other "have-to-memorize" material, most especially if it is set to rhythm, like poetry or rap. They like to use music to relax, to change their moods and are said to be deeply spiritual. Composers, conductors and musicians are obviously strong in musical intelligence, as are clergymen and spiritual healers, and those teens who are in their school band, play an instrument—or have formed or play in a band of their own!

_____ **Spatial or Visual Intelligence.** People with this intelligence can remember things well when they are put into picture form; they can memorize maps and charts. They like to see the whole picture all at once, rather than learning in bits and pieces. They use mental images and metaphors for learning. Architects, sculptors and pilots test high in this area, as do those teens who love classes in which they can express creativity. They are always doodling on their notebooks, or drawing "pictures" or symbols on their notes—whether it be class notes, or notes to friends or "someone special."

_____ **Kinesthetic or Physical Intelligence.** This is highly developed in athletes, dancers, gymnasts, and surgeons. Kinesthetically intelligent people have good control over their bodies and like to participate in sports, dance, and anything that requires movement. They have good timing, and are highly sensitive to the physical environment. These are people who learn best by doing, touching or moving objects around. Professional athletes would be identified as those having "kinesthetic" intelligence, as well as the teen who is consistently on a sports team in his or her school or community.

_____ **Interpersonal or People Intelligence.** A "people-person" relates well to others and understands the feelings of others. This is the teen who loves to join groups, is very social, a good communicator and does well in activities that require partners or teamwork. Salespeople, negotiators, motivational speakers and coaches are good examples of those high in interpersonal skills— as are those teens who are identified as "talkative" or "very social."

_____ **Intrapersonal or Intuitive Intelligence.** This intelligence is often called intuition. It is the ability to tap into information stored in the subconscious mind. Psychologists, hynotherapists, mystics and counselors show this type of intelligence. People who have intrapersonal intelligence are extremely interested in understanding the motives of people (what makes people tick)— including themselves. They are sensitive toward their own feelings, as well as the feelings of others. They are especially in touch with their own feelings, and are said to be "reserved" although they readily intuit (understand) what they learn and how it relates to others. They don't like to conform; they like to be independent and take control of their own learning. This is the teen who others come to when they have a broken heart or are uncertain, even confused, about their feelings.

_____ **Naturalist or Nature Intelligence.** A "nature" person loves the outdoors, animals and those things having to do with nature. This person is "in tune" with nature and is not likely to be afraid of spiders or other "creatures." He or she is likely to have a pet, whether it be a dog, cat, fish or reptile, and would prefer reading a book on the adventure of an animal as opposed to the adventure of a person. A volcanist (someone who studies volcanoes) exhibits nature intelligence, as does San Diego's world famous zoo ambassador Joan Embry, and the teen who saves a lizard (or mouse) from the jaws of his or her cat.

_____ **Philosophical or Existentialist Intelligence.** People of this intelligence ponder life in relationship to the "bigger picture"—such as demonstrating concern about the well-being of the planet, the world or the "world's citizens," or those who find meaning in being of service to humanity. Leaders—whether a president of a country, a "Mother Teresa" within a community, or a religious or spiritual leader—all qualify as having philosophical intelligence. The teen who leads a school or community drive to make the world—or community—a better place or who concerns himself with saving the rainforest or seeking his and others' "spiritual journey" also demonstrates this type of intelligence.

Again, no one of these nine is better than the others. All are good—all can indicate areas of talent and aptitude (or lack thereof). This information is good to know: It can help us set goals accordingly and point us in the direction of a job or career for which we may be well-suited. For example, if you love to play both the guitar and the flute, and learning to play them "just seemed to come naturally" to you, then you know the field of music will be an easy one for you to pick up. Having a talent for reading maps and drawing them to scale could mean that a career in the field of architecture might be just perfect for you.

You can also use this information to stop fretting about things you just don't ever seem to "get the hang of." For example, if you are not at all musically inclined, you may not want to take the time to learn a musical instrument. Sara Knorr obviously has a gift for organizing others into action and for getting things done. So probably Sara doesn't want to get a degree in computer programming, as much as getting one that allows her to explore managing people (personnel management) and fund-raising (financial management).

You can even use this information to set goals for turning a "weak area" into something you want to make stronger, such as learning more about or developing skills in an area in which you aren't so good but would like to be.

To give you an idea how you can use information about your aptitudes to set goals, we asked Sara Knorr to list her first, second and third strengths and tell us why she chose as she did. Here's her response:

#1 Interpersonal or People Intelligence: *I chose this one first because I'm a "people-person." I know that I relate well to others and understand their feelings. I love group activities (in fact, I love to start groups—and already started two at my school and one at my church). I'm very social, a good communicator, and I do great in activities that require partners or teamwork. Since salespeople, motivational speakers and coaches are good examples of those high in interpersonal skills, and I know that I'm good at selling others on my ideas and motivating them to take up my cause—as well as at coaching them through it—this has to be my strongest area.*

#2 Linguistic Intelligence: *I chose this area next because everyone agrees that I'm forever talking, and I can be very persuasive with words—both in letter-writing and when making speeches. I'm very systematic; I enjoy having a goal, and then seeing that it's met. And I'm a person who likes order. I can see that in my room—I like it neat and orderly. Even my closet is organized according to items, dresses, blouses, sweaters and things.*

#3 Intrapersonal or Intuitive Intelligence: *I'd say I'm not as strong in this area as the other two, but I chose it because I feel I'm intuitive (and I hope sensitive, although I can be impatient when things aren't getting done according to plan). I'm also very self-motivated. I'm aware of my strengths, like being able to organize others, and of my weaknesses, like not being at all mechanical. I also know that I'm the independent type.*

Next we asked Sara how she might use knowing about strengths and weaknesses in setting goals. Here is what she said:

Learning about the nine areas is useful for me in several ways. For example, I know for sure now that getting a degree in organizational and leadership skills would serve me better than getting a teaching certificate. My strongest area is in Interpersonal or People Intelligence, so I believe I'd be good at motivating and directing others to take action. I could be a social service agency's public-relations specialist or fund-raiser. I could train and manage staff, or do community outreach campaigns. (Of course, I'd choose to work for a program that helps children.)

   Since I also have Linguistic Intelligence, I could put my "way with words" to use in any of those jobs! Since I love to create order, I'd also be great as a program coordinator or director. And now that I can see that I'm not as sensitive to people's feelings as I thought I was, I want to get better at that.

List your first, second and third strengths, and explain why you chose them. Then, write what you feel this may tell you in terms of creating goals.

I'd list _____ as my #1 strength because: _____

_____

_____

_____

_____

I can use this information to set goals for myself, such as: _____

_____

_____

_____

_____

I'd list _____ as my #2 strength because: _____

_____

_____

_____

_____

I can use this information to set goals for myself, such as: ____

_____

_____

_____

I'd list _____ as my #3 strength because: _____

_____

_____

_____

_____

I can use this information to set goals for myself, such as: ____

_____

_____

_____

When you review the other areas, your numbers 4–9, how can you use what you discovered about yourself to set goals? (For example, Sara discovered that she wasn't as "sensitive to people's feelings" as she had thought, and because she knew she wanted to get better in this area, she set a goal to "strengthen" this "weakness.")

_____

_____

_____

_____

Having done this exercise on learning more about your aptitudes, did you discover something new about yourself, or is this pretty much what you knew all along? Explain.

_____

_____

_____

_____

_____

_____

Our strengths are often fairly obvious to others. Ask three people whose opinion you trust what it is they think that your talents and strengths are, as well as why they believe this to be so.

Who: _____

What the person said: _____

_____

_____

Who: _____

What the person said: _____

_____

_____

Who: _____

What the person said: _____

_____

_____

Look back over the statements others have made about you. Are there any similarities to what they say? For example, do their comments reflect that you are really good with people, or that you are best at getting things done on your own? Do they perceive you as being a stick-to-the-facts kind of person or do they see you as more of a creative "visionary" who stimulates ideas and sees things from a multifaceted point of view? Make a list of what, in general, others say about your aptitudes.

♥ _____

♥ _____

♥ _____

♥ _____

♥ _____

Looking over the list you've just created about what others said about your aptitudes, how might you best use this information to set goals? _____

_____

_____

_____

_____

_____

_____

In the coming chapters, you'll have a chance to examine how you can set goals and create a plan of action to further develop these aptitudes, as well as consider ways to use them.

It's Up to You!

Knowing your aptitudes is a powerful way to acknowledge—and appreciate—who you are. Another way to better know yourself lies in understanding how the things we love to do, our hobbies, show us a slice of "who we are." Because our hobbies allow us to express a particular talent or skill, they're a creative tool that brings us pleasure and satisfaction. What are your hobbies—and how can you use them to set goals for yourself? The next chapter will shed light on what's true for you!

6

Your Hobbies: Setting Goals That Explore Your "Innate" Interests

"All Dolled Up"

I had come downstairs ready to meet my new date! I was looking "hot"—if I do say so myself—or as my grandpa remarked (as he does whenever my sister, Elise, and I get dressed up), "all dolled up." Our grandfather lives with us, and we adore him. He's sweet, funny and just fun to be around. He teases us and we tease him—especially whenever he uses his ancient expressions, such as "all dolled up." We think "all dolled up" sounds funny, so we laugh and tell him thank you. Then whenever he puts on what he calls his "Sunday finest," we tell him he looks "hot"—but he doesn't get it, so we just say, "You look 'all dolled up,'" and he just laughs.

But funny thing about that saying of his, I'm now actually thinking of making "All Dolled Up" the name of my own business!

Ever since I was a little girl, I've had this thing about dolls. I mean, Elise did, too, but she didn't go to the extreme that I did. I considered my dolls really special—all of them—and kept them in perfect shape. Hers would become ratty over the months of wear and tear—hair all disheveled and faces dirty—and you can bet she always lost their tiny shoes and clothes, not to mention their little wigs, hats and hair accessories. Most of her dolls even ended up with missing limbs! Not mine. Even Elise commented that my dolls seemed to look better the longer I owned them. I'd make them little clothes and keep them immaculate. If they had hair, they ended up changing hairstyles as often as I did.

Eventually, Elisa moved on from dolls. She went through a stage of loving fish, then horses, and now, well, she's finally into boys! Dolls are not for my sister. She wouldn't be caught dead with one in her room, not even propped on top of her bookcase. This is not the case for me—I've never lost interest in my now vast collection of dolls. I went on to makeup and boys and a part-time job at a department store, but I still kept my prized doll collection in my room—and I've added more and more to it over the years. What's more, I began buying antique and collectible dolls. Some of them are complete wrecks, but I've found I have a very special knack for restoring them to picture perfection. I'll go out with my friends or my boyfriend on weekend nights, but I've always reserved every Saturday morning for scouring garage sales for valuable dolls in need of repair. I'll buy a nice "restorable" doll and fix it up and, if it isn't one I want to add to my own collection, I'll sell it. (I've made more money off my hobby than I have from any part-time job I've ever held.) Or sometimes I'll donate it to a charity—and they're able to sell the doll for a great deal of money. I feel like working with dolls is fascinating; it's an amazing thing to take a doll from complete disarray to utter beauty. I lose all sense of time when I'm working on my dolls. I like to believe that there isn't a doll I can't "resurrect" or give an awesome makeover. I even belong to an organization for doll collectors, and I get a monthly magazine. Once I sent in an article for consideration, and it was actually published. That was a few months back and now the magazine has offered me a regular column—and they will even pay me for it!

In a few months I start college, where I'm going to have a business major. I'm taking business courses so I can learn how to run a successful business, like a collector's doll shop, complete with departments for appraisal, restoration, and purchase and trading. It's right up my alley. I have no doubt that one day I will reach my goal of creating a business around the lucrative field of doll collection and restoration. I can't imagine doing anything else. As a child, if ever you wanted to find me, I'd be in my room with my head buried into working on my dolls. There's nothing I loved more, and I sometimes felt as if I could do it twenty-four hours a day! No one doubted it was my hobby, and because I love it so much, everyone agrees that it would be foolish not to make it my career goal. If you happen to see a sign on a shop that reads "All Dolled Up," it could mean that I've met my goal. You're welcome to stop on in and check it out!

Shana Nixon, 17

What a Hobby Reveals About You

It's obvious that Shana loves her hobby of collecting and restoring dolls—so much so that she loses all track of time while working on them. And, of course, now she plans on getting a college education centered on turning her hobby into a career. Hobbies are like that. Not only do they reveal what you find interesting, but they also shed light on who you are. Maybe you have a friend who collects stamps from various states and countries, while another friend has a "green thumb" who is interested in growing flowers, even "splicing" them to see if she can produce a hybrid plant from combining two from the same species. Then again, maybe she just gets satisfaction from taking care of a living thing and watching it bloom and grow. People can make hobbies of raising reptiles in terrariums or raising fish in aquariums. Some people get handheld metal detectors and make their hobby a hunt for buried treasures. Other people have some arts or crafts type of hobby—anything from needlepoint to decoupage, painting to sculpture. Then there are hobbies like collecting miniature furniture and building tiny homes and villages—the ideas are endless.

While you may think of your hobbies as "just for fun," a closer look can help you uncover another facet of "who you are"—revealing your true nature for what you find interesting and rewarding to do for work, such as a job or career. Again, all of it is useful information as you set about creating goals to bring you happiness, satisfaction and fulfillment.

Here are five good reasons to discover—and develop—your hobby.

1. **A hobby allows you to refine skills and develop new ones.** We asked Shana what skills she develops while engaged in her hobby. "I'd never consciously thought about all the skills I was using when I restored dolls," she told us, "until you asked me about them. I couldn't believe the 'skills workout' I was getting! Not only do I use skills of concentration while paying attention to all the detail involved in repairing cracks and painting on faces, but I use negotiation skills when I buy and sell my dolls. I also use more research skills than you can imagine, between shopping for parts and buyers and learning all I can about the market values for different dolls. I was amazed."

2. **Some hobbies may allow you some time alone—time to be with yourself.** Even if your hobby includes interacting with others (such as trading sports cards), it still allows you private moments with yourself. During this valuable time alone you are able to listen to your thoughts and mull over things going on in your life. This mental break away from your busy, competitive, day-to-day life gives you time to be peaceful. Alone time can be priceless. Remember Shana's sister, Elise? While she wasn't interested in dolls, Elise had

a hobby of her own. "I found my hobby when my grand-mother gave me an exquisite amaryllis plant," she told us. "I'd never had a plant of my own—and I never even gave my mom's garden a second thought. But there was something about that amaryllis that intrigued me." The instructions for caring for the plant explained that if Elise took proper care of the enormous bulb during blooming season, the bloom would be larger and last longer. It went on to suggest that under just the right conditions, the plant would bloom twice a year, rather than just the usual once. Of course, Elise decided she was going to "coax" the plant to be not only bigger, but also to bloom twice that year. When it did, Elise challenged it to grow still bigger yet! Elise now has five of the nine different colors (kinds) of amaryllis. "My goal is to own two more by the end of summer, and all nine by Christmas," Elise told us. She's also expanded her amaryllis hobby to include trying to cross her "Star of India" amaryllis with her "Rupert" amaryllis. "I have the stalks spliced and bandaged together," Elise explained, and then added, "I just love the time I spend taking care of my plants. I don't feel any pressure, and my mind can just wander anywhere it wants."

3. **A hobby allows you to discover things about yourself that you might never learn otherwise.** Hobbies give you those moments to get in touch with that part of yourself that wouldn't get expression otherwise. Elise said her hobby taught her she loves to nurture things and watch them grow—something she never would've known about herself if she hadn't been given that first amaryllis. Shana, on the other hand, told us her hobby showed her how much she likes to restore things to their original perfection. "Hobbies are so diverse," Shana added. "My boyfriend's hobby is cycling. Not only does he ride, but he also builds bicycles.

He says that riding has taught him that he loves to push himself physically, while building has taught him that he's creative—a word that he never would've used before to describe himself."

4. **A hobby allows you to set your own "standards of excellence."** So much in our culture coaches us to compete and compare ourselves with others. This isn't the case with a hobby; you get to excel to the level of your own choosing— you don't have to be better than someone else, nor are you held back to the level of another person. In your hobby, you are your own Einstein, van Gogh or Olympic gold medalist. As Elise reported, she doesn't feel any pressure; she just works on her amaryllis hobby for her own satisfaction— trying for extra blooms and experimenting with creating cross-breeds only for her own sense of achievement.

5. **Hobbies can reveal your true nature for work or a career.** Looking closely at what brings you great satisfaction can help you discover your talents, passions and aptitudes. We've seen how this worked for Shana, who has actually decided to make her hobby her life's work, but sometimes the direction your hobby gives you can be much more subtle. Elise, for example, doesn't want to raise amaryllis plants for a living—she wants to go to college to become a preschool teacher. Yet in that work she'll still have the opportunity to nurture and watch the children grow. Did you know that the hobby most plastic surgeons are drawn to is sculpting or painting? The attention to detail while creating a work of beauty appeals to them. And most race-car drivers, with their desire for speed and the thrill of overcoming danger, have hobbies like bungee jumping or parachuting. So while you may not make your hobby your life's work, it's important to listen to what it is telling you about your true nature for work. Why is this important? Because the expression of your hobby may be pointing you in the

direction of "making your joys your job, your toys your tools."

Do you have a hobby? If you do—and even if you don't— what could it say about you? The following exercise will help you find out.

VIRTUAL PRACTICE: YOUR HOBBY—AND HOW IT "DOLLS UP" YOUR LIFE

How would you define a hobby? Why do you think having a hobby is a good thing?

_____

_____

_____

Do you have a hobby? If so, what is it? How long have you had this hobby? What is it that you most enjoy about this hobby? Explain. (If you do not have a hobby, what hobby would you like to investigate most?)

_____

_____

_____

_____

Do you have more than one hobby? If so, what are the others? Does anyone you know have more than one hobby? Explain.

_____

_____

_____

Is this hobby something that you do alone, or are others involved in it? For example, is it a team sport, or are you cycling alone? Does your hobby require that you interact with others; for example, are you sharing information while trading baseball cards, or are you working silently on a woodworking project? Does the fact that you're alone or interacting with others play a part in your attraction to this hobby? Explain. (If you don't already have a hobby, explore in writing whether you would feel more drawn to hobbies that involve interaction or hobbies that you'd do alone.)

_____

_____

_____

_____

What achievements, awards or recognition have you received as a result of your hobby?

♥ _____

♥ _____

♥ _____

♥ _____

List all the skills that you can think of that are associated with your hobby. For example, when we asked Shana this question, she listed: concentration, researching, negotiating, problem-solving and creativity. (If you don't have a hobby, pick one that you'd like to learn more about and make a list of the skills you think it would help you to develop.)

♥ _____

♥ _____

♥ _____

♥ _____

♥ _____

Do you have a hobby that allows you to experiment or explore? How does it do this? How does experimenting help you set goals? For example, Shana's boyfriend gets to experiment with what bicycle parts would work best, and her sister Elise gets to experiment with whether or not she could cross ("splice") two different amaryllis plants to come up with a new hybrid (type).

_____

_____

_____

Do you collect stamps, baseball cards or something else? Or perhaps your hobby involves making something—like an art or craft, such as embroidery, decoupage or ceramics. List any arts and crafts you make or items that you collect.

_____

_____

_____

Maybe sports or some athletic activity is your hobby—such as cycling, aerobic dancing, handball, hiking, skating, swimming, volleyball, weight training or softball. List any sports or athletic hobbies you have or any of those kind of activities that you enjoy.

♥ _____

♥ _____

♥ _____

♥ _____

What skills do you think are related to having a sport or athletic activity as your hobby? Example: Having self-discipline or being a team player.

♥ _____

♥ _____

♥ _____

♥ _____

What can you learn in watching how others have turned their hobbies into something more than leisure-time activities? Talk to someone who has made his hobby also his work. This could be someone such as the baseball card shop owner if you collect baseball cards, a professional ball player if your hobby is softball or an artisan if you're into crafts. Ask him or her all about it. How did this person get started? What career opportunities does the hobby hold? Has it helped this person with goals he or she had in developing relationships? What about with developing goals in education? Write all that you learned from your "hobby expert."

_____

_____

_____

_____

What, if any, financial goals do you need to set for your hobby? Do you need to make ten dollars a month or seventy-five dollars a month to keep up your hobby? How will you earn that money?

_____

_____

_____

_____

_____

Because our hobbies are yet another indicator of who we are, be sure to set goals to explore them in depth. What we do for "fun" tells us something about ourselves. What goal would you like to set that can help you discover or develop your hobby?

_____

_____

_____

_____

_____

What other ways can you think of to use the information you've discovered about your hobby to shape goals for your life, now and in the future?

_____

_____

_____

_____

Maybe you think you don't have a particular hobby or any interest that could lead to one, but there are ways to find guidance in selecting a hobby. Think about those times when something you're doing captures your attention to the point that you lose all sense of time. At those times, what are you doing? Explain.

_____

_____

_____

_____

If you don't have a hobby, do you think that's a negative? Explain.

_____

_____

_____

_____

Where can you go, or whom can you turn to, to learn more about your hobby? For example, does your school counselor have books or resources that can help you? Be sure to ask! What about the Internet? Have you searched for Web sites that could direct you? Think of all the places you could go to gather more information. List your answers here. Example: I could take a weekend course at a junior college near me. (If you have no idea, be sure to list finding someone to ask for this information.)

♥ _____

♥ _____

♥ _____

♥ _____

If you're wondering what hobby is right for you, take a look at all the eBay offerings on the topic. Following you'll find a list of hobby ideas. As you read through them, see which ones stir an interest in you.

Collections: Antiques; Marbles; Dolls; Toys; Model Cars; Model Planes; Electric Trains; Baskets; Music (CDs, etc.); Memorabilia; Rocks; Gems; Shells; Angels; Fairies; Stuffed Animals; Sports Trading Cards

Arts and Crafts: Basketry; Beading (Jewelry); Candle Making; Incense Making; Ceramics; Pottery; Drawing; Painting; Calligraphy; Stained Glass; Mosaics; Leather Works; Crocheting; Knitting; Magic Tricks

Growing Things: Gardening; Flowers; Plants; Vegetables; Tropical Fish (Saltwater/Freshwater); Reptiles; Birds; Insects; Animals

Sports: Fishing; Flying Kites; Go-Carts; Cycling; Mountain Climbing; Mountain Biking; Surfing; Skateboarding; Skiing; Inline Skating; Hiking; Parasailing

This is just a partial list; hobbies and ideas for hobbies are practically limitless. We provide this list to help you get a feel for the different possibilities. Hopefully, even if you don't find one that's an exact fit, seeing some of what's available will inspire you to begin a search for a hobby that will be interesting and intriguing for you. If you're still having trouble deciding what hobby is right for you, try going to the library and exploring books on the subject. We like *The Teenager's Guide to Hobbies for Here and Now* by Norah Smaridge, but you will find many others as well.

It's Up to You!

As you can see, a hobby can play a big role in getting to know ourselves. Feeling that we know ourselves, liking the "face in the mirror," is the basis of self-esteem. And when we have a healthy self-esteem, we are more apt to set goals and accomplish them. Doing so leads to fulfillment. All it takes is knowing what you want.

So what do you want? In the next unit, you'll get a chance to find out!

Part 3

What Do You Want to Achieve—Today, Tomorrow and in the Future?

A vision sets direction for thinking and action.
—Edward de Bono

The future is purchased by the present.
—Samuel Johnson

*It is better to look ahead and prepare
than to look back and regret.*
—Jackie Joyner-Kersee

*The talents that you have are God's gift to you.
What you do with them is your gift to God.*
—Robert Schuller

*Great dances are not great because of their
technique; they are great because of
their passion.*
—Martha Graham

7

A Message from the Authors

Whereas the previous unit focused on discovering "who" you are, this unit will focus on the "what" you want—with a special emphasis on *empowering* you to "think big" as you explore goals to set for yourself. Each complements the other: "Knowing yourself" allows you to set goals that you will use and further develop your interests, talents and strengths. Setting and achieving goals that are "totally you" helps you to feel in touch with yourself and therefore in charge of your life. This, in turn, makes you feel happy, hopeful and fulfilled—which is an incentive to "think big."

Andrew Lufburrow certainly did! If we hit a rewind feature to take us back a year, we'd find Andrew asking his pre-calculus teacher for a break when his pager goes off for the third time. His teacher answers, "Hurry back." She knows the seventeen-year-old "CEO" is on his way to see a client. It was no secret among the faculty of C. Milton Wright High in Bel Air, Maryland, that Andrew had his own technology services business. Andrew earned a "C" in pre-calculus that year, but his company, AAL Technologies, turned in an "A+" performance, nearly tripling its size and quadrupling its revenue.

Fast-forward to the present: Andrew is now a freshman at the University of Maryland of Baltimore County (UMBC) where he continues to balance work and school. He has more than two dozen regular clients and, yes, he's taking calculus. Clients still buzz him during class, but his college professors understand his need to take care of business and are interested in seeing him succeed. After all, AAL Technologies is the first-ever student start-up to be headquartered in the school's new high-tech incubator, the UMBC Technology Center.

If Andrew can do it, you can, too! While Andrew's level of success may be exceptional for a teen, his ability is not. Teens everywhere are doing awesome and creative things. Like Andrew, you, too, can set goals to go after what you want. All it takes is knowing what "success" you're after, and a determination to go after what you want. Oh, and one other thing—you'll need a dream machine.

A "dream machine"? Yes, a dream machine. What "mechanism" do you use to think about all you want out of life? For example, do you hang around with interesting and creative friends who have big plans for their lives because being with them stimulates you to "think big"? Do you read broadly, exposing yourself to great minds because it expands your own sense of things? Do you attend classes and seminars to "stimulate" your thinking? Do you watch TV shows and films that are interesting and educational? Do you constantly observe others as they go about their lives, always evaluating if their lifestyle is one you'd like to emulate? Of course, these are not the only ways to "think big," but the point is, *Have you thought about what you want out of life, both now for the coming days and weeks, and for the months, even years, ahead?* This unit will help you answer that question so that in the coming chapters, you can set goals for the here and now—and for your future, as well. Doing so is a sure way to help you feel in charge of your life.

Speaking of being "in charge," are you willing to be in charge of your life, or is it a scary thought? Does being "in charge" feel to you like sixteen-year-old Brandon White of Westbrook, Maine, described it: "Cool, yet a little overwhelming, too"? We asked Brandon to elaborate. Here's what he said: "On some days I feel really in control—which is a feeling I like. I especially feel 'in charge' at times like when I've prepared for my classes and it really paid off; I'm called on in class, and I can answer a question intelligently. I feel 'in charge' when I get to use the family car and drive myself to and from school. I feel 'in charge' when I've just deposited a portion of my paycheck from my part-time job into my savings account to go toward buying a car of my own, going to college and other things. But there are also times when I'm just glad that I'm living with my parents, and all I have to do is focus on doing well for the day at hand—like when I'm browsing for a car I can afford to buy, or comparing car insurance or looking over the tuition and fees to get into a college and thinking I'll be in debt forever. So, I'd have to say that while I'm feeling really 'in charge' on some days, at other times I'm happy to know I still have a little time before I have to actually be completely responsible for all the decisions that I know are mine to eventually make. But I do have big plans for myself, because I want to be a success—I mean, I consider myself a success now, but I want to be a success in the *real world*, too."

How about you? Do you want to be a success? Whether you are at the stage of having wishes but not as yet having turned them into goals, or whether you're able to identify an entire list of things you'd like to accomplish, either way, consider this unit a source to rev up your "go for it" battery. This can surely help you be a success in the "real world."

Well, okay then! Now that you're ready to be a success in the "real world," let this unit motivate you to get your dream machine in place! We know you're a taste berry—and taste-berry teens take charge of their lives! Here's hoping that your dream machine gets you everything you want!

Taste Berries to You! Bettie and Jennifer Leigh Youngs

8

How Do You Define Success?

What Do Brittany Whiteside, Chris Burke and Lyle Rincon Have in Common?

Brittany Whiteside

By the time she was thirteen years old, Brittany Whiteside dreamed of knowing her way around the Internet. She didn't even know exactly what it was she'd find there, but she was curious to find out. Creative Web pages especially caught her eye. Whenever Brittany spotted what she considered "an awesome Web page with an effect that was fun or a layout that was cool," she would take note of the source code. Then step-by-step she'd go through the source code so she could re-create it for herself later. By the time she was fifteen years old, Brittany had started her first Web site—one little page, with her hobby of beaded jewelry as its topic! Then, she decided her site would carry an array of beads from different wholesalers, instructions for re-creating beads, patterns pages on the history of beads and beautiful pictures of exquisite beadwork. Her one-page Web site now had four pages. She founded her company, "String Along"—with its ever-expanding Web site—and the rest is, as they say, "history"!

Today Brittany's site averages about forty-two hundred page views per day. It's grown into a huge archive, not only filled with everything Brittany had dreamed of, but also including listings of where to purchase nearly a thousand different kinds of beads, as well as one hundred bead-working patterns. It also posts two hundred pieces of beaded jewelry, beading tools and supplies, and all sorts of other beadwork items. Though Brittany is set to begin college in the fall, her lucrative company (like its creator) will remain, as she likes to put it, "stringing along," ever forward on the road to success.

Chris Burke

Chris Burke was born with Down's syndrome. Children born with this syndrome have one too many chromosomes, resulting in a similar appearance, thwarted development and a ceiling on potential. Since IQ peaks out at around 75, capability and ability are severely limited—or so it was thought.

Most of the world now knows Chris Burke not only from his unforgettable interview on national television some years ago when he came in third in the Special Olympics—and wowed the world with his "acceptance" speech—but also as the charismatic and gifted actor and television star of the television series, *Life Goes On*. The show enjoyed four years of excellent ratings. He's also authored a bestselling book, *A Special Kind of Hero*, and is currently the editor-in-chief of the National Down's Syndrome Society magazine, devoting tireless energy to making his new dream come true—helping create a magazine to expand awareness and understanding of Down's syndrome. Chris offers some words on why he thinks this very special and much-needed national magazine is so successful: "We're successful because we talk about what works. We don't dwell on the negatives. We highlight victories!"

This very special young man has surged well beyond the commonly held assumptions of those with Down's syndrome.

Interestingly it is not outside the scope of what he expects of himself. "I grew up with being told not to place limitations on myself," he says. "My parents taught me to always 'upgrade my expectations' and to set goals for a great life. My motto is: 'Find something you love to do, set goals for achieving it, and be willing to spend the time it takes to accomplish it.' That's the key to success. When you're doing what you like to do, it puts a smile on your face!" Chris adds, "I want to produce and direct a movie next. It's just a matter of time." Suddenly his eyes light up and he says, "I'd love to do a movie with Steven Spielberg. . . . Seriously, he's the very best director there is. He's my mentor: I want to be as good a director as he is." Laughing like a grizzly bear gargling through honey, Chris adds, "Someday, I will." Given his track record for goal-setting and achievement, we have no reason to doubt that Chris will do that, too.

Lyle Rincon

By the age of eighteen, Lyle Rincon's life was spiraling out of control. Lyle had started drinking with friends, "just to party" on weekends when he was in the ninth grade, but by the time his senior year rolled around, Lyle was drinking on a regular basis, sometimes even before school in the morning. "When I got arrested for being under the influence of alcohol at a concert," Lyle told us, "I thought it was the worst thing that could ever happen to me. But now I can see I wasn't only arrested; I was actually rescued." Lyle was court-ordered into an alcohol awareness program where he learned about alcoholism, about himself and about how to live a life of sobriety. "I learned so much. One day at a time, I know I can live a successful life sober. Now, there are so many things I want to achieve. One of my most important goals is to become an alcohol awareness educator teaching DUI classes," Lyle explains. "While I never ended up with a DUI, I know that's where I was headed—and I'd like to help others who weren't as lucky as I was. I know firsthand how helpless and desperate being addicted to alcohol can make you feel—and I know firsthand that there's a way out."

With more than two years of sobriety, Lyle is now enrolled in college where he's completing courses to become certified as an alcohol and drug counselor. He volunteers at the outpatient program that he was once court-ordered to attend and has an internship at a "teen recovery center" in his area. "Right now success means two things to me: continuing to stay sober one day at a time (that's the biggest one), and two, to have a full-time career as an alcohol awareness educator." Already quite a success in his recovery, Lyle is well on his way to achieving his new goals.

What Makes a Person Successful?

In the stories above, which teen do you consider to be the "most successful"? Would you say that it was Lyle Rincon, who overcame alcoholism and was then moved to create a career of helping others around his experience? Or would you consider it Brittany Whiteside, who launched a hugely successful Web-based business of her very own and made an enormous amount of money in the process? Perhaps your idea of the greatest success is Chris Burke, who not only soared well beyond what is considered possible for someone born with Down's syndrome, but whose achievements are extraordinary for anyone his age?

So who is the most successful? It depends. What one person sees as success is not always the same as what the next person perceives it to be. To some, being a success may mean making a lot of money, while to another it may be winning a tough competition, and to yet another it could be overcoming a seemingly insurmountable obstacle. To someone else, "being successful" may be seen as having attained material things—such as a fancy car, their "dream home" or owning nicely tailored clothes—while for another it's having earned the recognition, admiration, and love of friends and family. For still others, it may be "peace of mind" or being healthy and feeling energetic and able to do the things the person wants to do. Success might even be perceived as an achievement, such as having lowered a sprint time, raised a math score, earned a college diploma or secured a position.

You can define success in many ways. Do you wonder why defining success is important? Knowing what you consider the mark of success for you helps you set your goals to reach that success. Overall, we could say Chris Burke's definition of a successful life was not to limit his possibilities. He had quite a lot of success goals met along the way to succeeding at his life-goal. Chris first viewed success as finishing the race at the Special Olympics, and he then made that the goal he raced toward achieving. Next, he saw success as having a starring role in a television series, and that became the goal he set for himself and achieved. Then, there was authoring the book, helping create the magazine, and now he's added directing to his definitions of success. Each time, each definition of what "success" would look like secured his placement of his goals and his course toward achieving them.

Lyle Rincon's definition of success is to help others understand and overcome alcoholism. Knowing this, Lyle has a direction for setting goals to secure a career in that field. Brittany Whiteside once defined success as being able to create her own Web site—we can see how her definition of success expanded, right along with the goals she set and achieved, all the way up to running her own successful Web-based business. Defining success helps you figure out where it is you want to go so that you can then set goals to get you there. So the question is, *What is your definition of success?* The following exercise will help you define it for yourself.

VIRTUAL PRACTICE:
I'LL BE A SUCCESS WHEN I . . .

To me, "being a success" means:

_____

_____

_____

_____

I'll consider myself a "success" when:

_____

_____

_____

_____

Who is the most successful person you know, and why would you say this person is a success?

_____

_____

_____

_____

Name a success you have had in the last month. What goals did you set for achieving it?

_____

_____

_____

_____

Take a moment to think about your three biggest successes in life to date. What are they? Describe each one.

_____

_____

_____

_____

_____

_____

_____

What do these "successes" tell you about your definition of "success"?

_____

_____

_____

How will being "successful" make you different from how you are now? In what ways will you be different? Explain.

_____

_____

_____

_____

What one thing would you like to do or learn but haven't yet tried? What keeps (or prevents) you from accomplishing this?

_____

_____

_____

_____

It's Up to You!

As you can see, your definition of success is all your own. It's important in that it becomes your "blueprint" for setting those goals that will get you from here to there. Whether you're building a birdhouse or a castle, it will be helpful to have the right set of blueprints—the right goals.

Speaking of castles, have you ever wondered if you are dreaming big enough? This next chapter will help you create a "dream machine" big enough to go after your grandest dreams of success—which, of course, is exactly the way taste-berry teens would have it.

9

Are You Dreaming "Big Enough"?

Are You *Afraid* to Be "... Gorgeous, Talented, Fabulous"?

I really wanted to run for class office at my school. Winning would be so great—but losing, well, if I didn't win, I'd be the "loser." I went back and forth between "go for it" and "don't do it," wondering what to do. Then, in the middle of trying to get beyond my "fear of losing," I saw a poster with the words of author Marianne Williamson, where she makes the point that "our deepest fear is not that we are inadequate" . . . but rather, "our deepest fear is that we are powerful beyond measure." She believes that people say they want to be "gorgeous, talented and fabulous," but they're afraid to be. Yet we have every right to those qualities since, she says, we are "a child of God" and "playing small doesn't serve the world." In other words, letting your light shine is what you're supposed to do. Her words stopped the battle going on in my head; I decided right then and there to "Go for it!" But her words also made me think about whether I had really been afraid of losing—or afraid that I might win! Was I afraid I'd be in the position of having to save face, or showing my face (leading)? As I was searching for an answer to my question, I remembered her advice to "let your light shine" and that, in doing that, we give others the "permission to do the same." That poster made me a fan of Marianne Williams that day—and a campaigner for the office of class president!

Corey Richards, 17

Your "Dream Machine": Don't Leave Home Without It

Corey isn't alone in his admiration for Marianne's words. We agree wholeheartedly with Corey's enthusiasm over Marianne Williamson's beautiful words, which come from her book, *A Return to Love*. It's reported that the great visionary, Nelson Mandela, was so taken by Marianne Williamson's point in our not playing "small" that he used her words in his message to the world following his inauguration as president of South Africa. Looking at his life, one can see how he embodied that message: Having been imprisoned for decades for his stand against apartheid, he was released to become the first black president of the very nation that had imprisoned him! Marianne's words became his dream—a grand and glorious vision he aspired to in his ongoing fight for human rights for his people and his country—one he realized only because he refused to "play small" and dared to dream big!

What about you? Is your desire to be "brilliant, gorgeous, talented and fabulous"? How will you ensure that you don't "play small," "shrink," or "feel insecure"? What are your plans so that you "manifest all that is within" and "let your own light shine"? How will you become "powerful beyond measure"? Aside from believing that all is possible, you'll need to set goals to live your life accordingly.

Having a vision for what you want, your ideal and where

you're headed is an important part of making a dream come true. Perhaps you have a pretty good idea about what you'd like to accomplish this week, this month or in the coming semester. Maybe you've even got things pretty much figured out for the coming year. But what about for your future?

The future always seems so far away, but it's not really. Consider the quote, "Nothing is so far away as yesterday." The truth is, your future begins again every moment. So get in the habit of thinking about your future as tomorrow—and not some nebulous date in the way-off land of years and years from now. Is your dream machine—right now—busy working on the dreams you want to accomplish for your future? It should be.

When you see your future, what do you see? It's helpful to create a vision in your mind's eye of your future. The section below will help you do just that.

VIRTUAL PRACTICE: CREATING A VISION FOR *YOUR* FUTURE

For each of the groups of questions below, picture yourself at twenty-five years of age. At the end of each question, ask yourself: "What goals did I have to meet to get here?" Okay, go ahead and do this exercise, and as you do, don't forget to dream big!

My "Future" Life

Where are you living—in what city and state?

City: _____   State: _____

Are you renting an apartment, or buying a condo or house? What does your home look like? How big is it? Is it small or large? Is it one bedroom, two or three? What is the color of your carpet—or do you have stone or wood flooring? Describe your furniture, the pictures on the walls and your furnishings.

_____

_____

_____

_____

What sort of car are you driving? What is the year, make and model? Did you buy your car or are you leasing it?

_____

_____

_____

_____

What are you doing for work? Did you graduate from college and are you in your first job? Did you go to trade school and been in the workforce for a couple of years? Are you working for a company (large or small?) or for yourself? Are you paid by the hour or do you have a salary? How much do you earn a year? Do you have a savings account, checking account and credit cards?

_____

_____

_____

_____

_____

_____

_____

Are you working toward an even greater degree in education? What kind of classes are you taking for personal enrichment? How do you see yourself learning and growing—in what areas do you continue to study?

_____

_____

_____

_____

_____

Who are your friends? Are they the same faces from junior high and high school, or are they mostly new friends you've made at work and in your personal life, like working out at the gym, shopping and in your leisure-time activities?

_____

_____

_____

_____

What kind of organizations or associations do you belong to? Are you involved in a club, business organization or church group? What memberships do you hold? Are you an officer—or aspiring to an office—in any of these affiliations?

_____

_____

_____

_____

Do you work out regularly? Do you belong to your local gym or workout center? How often do you work out? Are you in good shape? Are your friends into fitness? What kind of activities are you involved in to stay fit?

_____

_____

_____

_____

_____

Do you enjoy cooking at home or do you eat out as often as you can? What sorts of restaurants do you go to? Do you often have friends over for meals? Do they join you in the kitchen and help you cook the meal, or do you have the meal prepared ahead of time?

_____

_____

_____

_____

How do you spend your weekends? What do you do for fun? Do you go fishing or hiking? Do you go to movies? Is the beach the place you'd like to relax, or do you prefer the pool? How often do you go on vacation, and how is your vacation spent?

_____

_____

_____

What are your hobbies? How often do you find the time to enjoy your hobby? Has your hobby also become something you do for work?

_____

_____

_____

_____

_____

_____

Do you live alone or with a roommate? If you live with someone, how did you meet? What sort of person is he or she? What does he or she look like? What sort of a job does he or she have? Did that person graduate from college? Do the two of you share the same values? Do you have the same friends? Do you work out together and socialize together? Do you have pets?

_____

_____

_____

_____

_____

_____

Are you single, dating, engaged or married? Describe the person you are dating (or married to). What does he or she look like? What sort of a job does he or she have? Did that person graduate from college? Do you already have kids? If not, do the two of you plan to have children and, if so, how many? Do you plan to send them to a public school, a private school, or home-school them?

_____

_____

_____

_____

_____

_____

_____

What do you do for spiritual fulfillment? Do you set aside a regular time to pray or meditate? Do you read spiritual or inspirational literature? Do you belong to one church, or go to various churches? Are you practicing the faith you practiced when living with your parents?

_____

_____

_____

_____

_____

_____

_____

Did you find this exercise intriguing? Most teens do. Thinking about your future now allows you to plan for it—to "make it happen"—which is what setting goals is all about.

It's Up to You!

Your dreams are those visions of success that pull you forward as you meet your goals. But even great dreamers need more than imagination to achieve their goals. They also need to believe in their dreams—as well as take responsibility for being "in charge" of completing whatever action is necessary to make those dreams come true. As Ugo Betti's great quote suggests, *"When you want to believe in something, you also have to believe in everything that's necessary for believing in it!"*

Are you ready and willing to be in charge? The next chapter will help you decide if you have what it takes!

10

Are You Willing to Be in Charge of Your Life?

I Am, I Can, I Will

I AM—two small words, and yet,
It's a powerful "place" in which to be.
It's my life, and I'm living it,
I am everything you see.

I am responsible for my actions,
And all the things I say and do.
I am responsible for my behavior,
And how I interact with you.

I am responsible for the level of my work,
And the choices that I make.
I am responsible for the values I profess,
And for the ways that I communicate.

I CAN—two small words, and yet,
It's a powerful "place" in which to be.
It's my life, and I'm living it,
Traveling the land, sky and sea.

I can earn the respect of others,
And gain their friendship true.
I can honor all things living, and
Take care of my mind, health and body, too.

I can do my best each day,
And I can know my best is great.
I can continue to progress,
And move closer to my fate.

I WILL—two small words, and yet,
It's a powerful "place" in which to be.
It's my life, and I'm living it,
I will be everything, just wait and see.

I will use my talents wisely,
Learn to manage the moods of life.
I will respect my ups and downs,
Ask for help in overcoming strife.

"I will" is a promise to see clearly;
It reveals my strength to win,
As I arrive at mutual resolutions,
And look for my answers from within.

I'm young, still learning, growing, changing,
Yet I have ideals, noble goals and plans,
For things like a healthy environment,
World peace and a crime-free land.

No longer a child, yet not an adult,
I am a teenager still.
But don't underestimate my value,
Because I am, I can and I will.

Jennifer Leigh Youngs
from Taste Berries for Teens

Are You Taking Responsibility for Your Life?

You are, as Jennifer so aptly states in her poem, "still learning, growing, changing," yet you are well on your way to becoming an adult. Naturally, this means that very soon you're going to have more say in the things you do and in the choices you make. Having more control of your life means more than just lifestyle choices—such as staying up later or spending even more time with your friends. It means that almost everything is up to you: You are responsible for your health and well-being, for planning the events of your days and seeing things through to completion, for planning your future and doing those things that will bring about your goals and desires. In short, growing up is about taking responsibility for you.

Taking responsibility means that you can read the previous poem and say, "Me, too." It means thinking of yourself as being the architect of your own life. You design the plans, draw up the blueprints and oversee the construction. Of course, you don't do all of the construction yourself. Your parents, family, teachers and others help "build" you; obviously, their influence helps shape the person you will become. But in the final analysis, what happens is up to you. Others will help, but it is your plan, your dream to be built.

Are you *managing* your life? Are YOU shaping the direction of your life? Or, are you letting others do it? The following section will give some clarity on how you feel about this.

VIRTUAL PRACTICE:
TAKING CHARGE (OF YOUR LIFE)

How do you feel about your life right now? Are you "happy" with it, or is there something you would like to change? Explain.

_____

_____

_____

Would you say that your life is relatively exciting, or would you describe it as dull, boring, routine? Explain. If you feel like your life needs change in this area, what could you do to change it?

_____

_____

_____

_____

Would you say that you are in control of your life, or do you feel like others have more say in the things that happen to you than you do? Explain.

_____

_____

_____

_____

List two areas of your life in which you feel you have total control, and explain how this is so. What's your part in owning this control?

♥ _____

_____

_____

_____

♥ _____

_____

_____

_____

List two areas of your life in which you feel you have little or no control, and explain why you know this is so. What, if anything, could you do to take charge in these areas—or are they better left to the care of others?

♥ _____

_____

_____

♥ _____

_____

_____

Would you say that you're a person who sets goals, or that you more or less let things happen randomly? Explain.

_____

_____

_____

Has the fear of failure or being criticized ever affected your ability to set and achieve goals? Explain.

_____

_____

_____

How can having a plan of action give you more *control* over all areas of your life?

_____

_____

_____

Would you say that you know yourself pretty well? Explain how this knowledge or lack of it can help you take responsibility for your life and your goals.

_____

_____

_____

It's Up to You!

Feeling like you're "in charge" of your life is a terrific feeling. When you're ready and willing to take responsibility for creating success and living your dreams, you are in the perfect place to set those goals and implement the right plan of action to assure that you achieve them. Now's the time for you to "take charge" and press on toward your prized goals. As we move into the next unit, you'll find a step-by-step course to help you reach them.

READER/CUSTOMER CARE SURVEY

We care about your opinions. Please take a moment to fill out this Reader Survey card and mail it back to us.

As a special "thank you" we'll send you exciting news about interesting books and a valuable **Gift Certificate.**

Please PRINT using ALL CAPS

First Name		MI.	Last Name	

Address

City		ST	Zip	

Phone # (____) ____ — ____   Fax # (____) ____ — ____

Email

(1) Gender:
____ Female   ____ Male

(2) Age:
____ 8 or younger   ____ 17-20
____ 9-12   ____ 21-30
____ 13-16   ____ 31+

(3) What attracts you most to a book?
(Please rank 1-4 in order of preference.)

	1	2	3	4
3) Title	○	○	○	○
4) Cover Design	○	○	○	○
5) Author	○	○	○	○
6) Content	○	○	○	○

(7) Other than school books, how many books do you read a month?
____ 1   ____ 3
____ 2   ____ 4

(8) How did you find out about this book?
Please fill in ONE.
1) ____ Friend
2) ____ School (Teacher, Library, etc.)
3) ____ Parent
4) ____ Store Display
5) ____ Teen Magazine
6) ____ Interview/Review (TV, Radio, Print)

(9) Where do you usually buy books?
Please fill in your top TWO choices.
1) ____ Bookstore
2) ____ Religious Bookstore
3) ____ Online
4) ____ Book Club/Mail Order
5) ____ Price Club (Costco, Sam's Club, etc.)
6) ____ Retail Store (Target, Wal-Mart, etc.)

(11) Did you receive this book as a gift?
____ Yes   ____ No

(12) What do you like to read? *(Please check all that apply)*

Magazines:
12) ____ Teen People
13) ____ Seventeen
14) ____ YM
15) ____ Cosmo Girl
16) ____ Rolling Stone
17) ____ Teen Ink
18) ____ Christian Magazines

Books:
19) ____ Fiction
20) ____ Self-Help Books
21) ____ Reality Stories/Memoirs
22) ____ Sports
23) ____ Series Books (Chicken Soup, Fearless, etc.)

TAPE IN MIDDLE; DO NOT STAPLE

BUSINESS REPLY MAIL
FIRST-CLASS MAIL PERMIT NO 45 DEERFIELD BEACH, FL

POSTAGE WILL BE PAID BY ADDRESSEE

TASTE BERRIES™ FOR TEENS
3201 SW 15TH STREET
DEERFIELD BEACH FL 33442-9875

FOLD HERE

(24) Do you prefer to read books written by:
1) ____ Teen Authors?
2) ____ Adult Authors?
3) ____ No Preference

Comments:

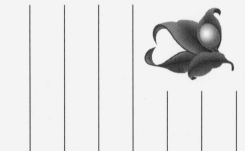

Part 4

Ready, Set, Go! Your Personal Guide to Creating Goals

It's not accident or time or fortune that keeps you from the things you want, but rather, your own thinking.
—Lillian Hellman

When you want to believe in something, you also have to believe in everything that's necessary for believing in it.
—Ugo Betti

The goal is to make your joys your job, your toys your tools.
—Jennifer Leigh Youngs

Take charge of your life! To act intelligently and effectively, we must have a plan. To the proverb which says, "A journey of a thousand miles begins with a single step," I would add the words, "and a road map."
—Cecile M. Springer

I finally figured out the best reason to be alive is to enjoy it.
—Rita Mae Brown

11

A Message
from the Authors

Taking into account your interests, talents and aptitudes, combined with having created a vision of your future, you now have a good starting point for setting goals you'll find stimulating, exciting and worth achieving. This is true for going after the things you want now, such as good friends, good grades, playing sports, a great family life and time for yourself, as well as for what you want in the near future, such as going to college, getting a job and living on your own. Shaping the direction of your life is not only inspiring, but also motivating! And like we said, so much of it is up to you!

Remember, though, that what you do and the goals you put in place right now connect you to your future, so don't wait to get started on creating your dreams. Start now. Just as attending practice on a regular basis on the sports field equates to improved performance come game day, and consistently working for good grades each year equates to a better chance to graduate with good marks, setting goals and having a plan to achieve them is the surest path to being successful in bringing about the life you want.

Again, up to now, you've been focused on thinking a lot about yourself and understanding more fully how you can take responsibility for bringing about the life you want. It's time to forge ahead. In this unit, you'll get a chance to become really proficient in setting goals and developing a plan of action to make that happen. You'll see how having a plan for achieving your goals is as important as the goals themselves. Maybe you want to buy a used car, pass a particular final, save for college, get your parents to agree on a longer curfew, or maybe you have some other objective. As you'll learn in this unit, while creating a goal is an important first step, desire alone isn't going to bring results. You need a strategy, a carefully laid plan, to bring about your desired outcome. Without a plan, you run the risk of letting things happen randomly, by chance or by accident. And if you just go along letting life happen at will, you never know how things will turn out. Maybe it will be just fine and you'll be happy with any outcome—be it job, friends, your living arrangements and the like. But maybe it will not be to your liking, and you'll feel disappointed, short-changed—or worse. Probably you've heard any number of people say, "If only I had . . ." Don't let yourself get caught in the "shoulda, coulda, woulda" category. Planning is the key to getting what you want.

You "direct" the outcome of your life by the things you do—and don't do—each and every day. So have a plan. If you don't anticipate ahead of time what you are going to wear to school tomorrow, you might get up and find that a favorite item or outfit needs to be laundered and therefore you'll have to choose something else—something that is not "the look" for which you hoped. But if you plan ahead, you can see if your clothes are clean and ready to wear. If you are taking a friend to a birthday dinner at his or her favorite restaurant, and you don't call ahead for reservations, you may get there and find that you cannot be seated (or arrive and find you've chosen the one day the restaurant is closed). Of course, by planning ahead, you can avoid these things. So don't "run" your life in a haphazard manner.

A plan to achieve your goals serves as your map, showing you the exact route for getting to your destination—which is succeeding in accomplishing your goals. First you'll learn the ten "rules" for creating goals, guidelines that will increase your chances of following through on achieving the things you'd like to accomplish. Then, you'll get a chance to formulate goals in nine specific categories—which is sure to help you feel like you're living life to its fullest! Finally, you'll learn how to create a plan of action so as to achieve each of those goals, and see how doing so is a terrific way to manage your time.

And speaking of managing your time (always a huge issue with teens), how are you doing it? Do you feel you're meeting your schedule, or do you often feel behind or overwhelmed? Do you seem to never have enough time? If not having enough time seems to be a problem for you, why do you think this is so? Do you think it's because you simply have too much to do, or is it because of the way you prioritize your activities? Do you lose control over getting things done when they need to be accomplished? Or do you sometimes procrastinate, putting things off until the last minute, until you are faced with the mad rush to get things done? If you constantly battle with knowing what needs to be done now as opposed to what can be done later, or even much later, not to worry. This unit will help you set goals, and then learn how to break your nine overall goals into monthly, weekly and daily "to-do's," so that you can do all that you need to in order to achieve them. So think of this as "Goal Map Drafting 101" as you draw up a step-by-step guide for creating great goals. Then with your map in hand, you can set off on the road to success in meeting your goals.

Okay, then, are you ready? If so, get set and let's go!

Taste Berries to You! Bettie and Jennifer Leigh Youngs

12

"The Rules" for Designing Goals (You'll Commit To)

This Year, Things Are Going to Be (Really) Different!

This next year, I'm going to do things a lot differently than I did last year. I know I said this last year, but having really blown it, I am absolutely positively sure I'm changing my ways this next school year. And for good reason!

Last year as I was getting ready to go into ninth grade, I thought, *Okay, this is my first year being in high school, and I want to get off to a good start. I'm going to be cool this year, and I'm going to accomplish some things. I want to make a lot of great friends and have everyone at school think of me as someone who's really got it together. I'm going out for sports; I'm going to find a cool boyfriend; be elected as an officer of my class; and please my parents by getting good grades. I want to look and act cool. I especially want to grow my hair long, and I'm going to work out to my aerobics video every single day.*

I had some other goals, too. For example, I'd promised myself, *No more swearing,* and just to make sure I wouldn't, I decided I would stop hanging around with Randee Hogan. Not only does she cuss all the time, but she's a big gossip and I should know: Last year I'd gotten in more than my share of sticky situations by getting caught up in the rumors she started—like the one about Sierra Gould making out with Tristin Tyler. You can't believe how much my reputation was tarnished because I hung around with her (and because everyone knew the rumor wasn't true). So I knew some changes were in order, and now that I'd become a ninth-grader, I decided that there would be no more spreading gossip and rumors for me, because I had decided that it was "out" with Randee, and "in" with Shandra Gregory and Wendy Tomposa—the best-liked and most-respected girls at school. To all these great intentions, I'd start doing something really cool with my soon-to-be-long, flowing hair—which is really saying something, since my hair is, as my best friend says, a "problem child with a mind of its own."

My ninth-grade year started, and before I knew it, it was over, and quite frankly, I didn't know whether to laugh or cry at how it turned out. First of all, I spent the whole year waiting for Nathan Baker to notice me, and what a waste of time that was! He didn't even notice that I was alive—although Lenny Stone did. He asked me out, but I said "no," which was a dumb decision because he's cool and one of the best-liked guys in the school. (I was just holding out for Nathan.) I wasted my entire year waiting for Nathan and only Nathan—who was dating Sara Goldman, a girl two years older than he. I was so sure that sooner or later, they'd break up—but they're still together.

On the matter of my grades . . . well, my parents were hardly deliriously happy with them—although I was happy just to pass: It seemed like there was one homework assignment on top of another, and I was always behind and turning assignments in late on a regular basis—which got me a lower grade every time, so I'm just glad I'm going into tenth grade! As for my working out, well, I broke out the aerobics videotape all of three times the entire school year; I never did decide on a new hairstyle; and as for my friendships with Shandra and Wendy, well, they're still waiting to be developed. With my keeping tabs on Nathan and his girlfriend, and constantly checking around on the status of their relationship, I lost a lot of precious time. I guess you could say that was true for the time I spent with Randee, too. I ended up hanging around with her for most of the year, so my goal of not hanging out with her and instead spending time with "nicer" friends bit the dust—as did most of all my other goals. At least I still managed to cut down on the swearing a little bit.

So, in my ninth-grade year, I didn't get all of the things accomplished that I'd hoped. Now as I'm getting ready to go into the tenth grade, I'm not going to leave things to "hope." This year I'm going to write my goals down and put them where I can see them. After last year—when the time just got away from me—this year I plan to be very serious about making sure things happen according to plan!

Cammie Brinthall, 15

"The Rules": Ten Guidelines for Designing Goals

Do you, like Cammie, start out with great intentions, but then get sidetracked from accomplishing the things you want to get done? It can happen. But it's a lot less likely to happen if you have a plan for achieving the things you want to accomplish. With a plan, things aren't left to chance. If you know the direction in which you should head, you know where to focus your time and energy. Channeling your efforts in a specific direction can keep you on track to getting what you want, to bringing your intentions to fruition.

But although goals may start out as hopes, dreams, desires, intentions or ambitions, they are more than wishful thinking. Goals are concrete plans. Here are ten "rules" for creating goals, guidelines that will increase your chances of following through on achieving the things you'd like to accomplish. (In the coming chapters, you'll get a chance to learn more about each of these, and create a plan of action that leads to your achieving your goals.)

Here are the ten "rules":

1. **Put your goals in writing.** Writing out your goals helps you examine them and see what they really are. Doing this can help you commit to them. Once you've written out those things you'd like to "do, be, have and achieve," you have a "map" reminding you of where you wish to be—and when you wish to arrive there. Knowing when and where you want to be helps you develop a plan so you know how best to spend your time and energy. This can help you stay on track toward accomplishing the things you want to achieve. A plan points you in the direction of what it is you should be doing each month, week and day to move closer to your goal. And best of all, with a written plan, you can readily see all you are doing. You can measure how far you've come, and when you are off-course. Then you can get back to doing those things that move you in the direction of meeting your goals. Notice that Cammie, in the story at the beginning of this chapter, had many goals, but she never wrote them down. As you can see, the goals she professed became merely good intentions. If Cammie had written down her goals, her intentions would have been transformed into a plan of action, and as a result, she would have had a better chance at goal achievement.

2. **Be sure your goal is clear and specific.** Goals that are specific, as opposed to those that are ambiguous, are easier to tackle. State your goals clearly and be specific. For example, rather than saying, "I need to make some money," say, "I need to make at least sixty-five dollars each month between now and Christmas." If Cammie had selected one specific sport, rather than just saying, "I want to go out for sports," she would have had a better chance of knowing precisely

when she needed to "sign up and show up" to begin achieving her goal. As it was, her goal was never clear: She didn't clarify what sport she wanted to go out for, and the result was that Cammie had no direction—no beginning and no end. She never did become part of any sports team during her ninth-grade year. If you don't decide a direction in which to go, it's unlikely you'll reach your desired destination. Certainly this was true for Cammie in her ninth-grade school year.

3. **"Own" your goal(s).** When you set a goal, ask, "Is this goal really important to *me*?" If you don't really "buy into" your goal—if you don't really want to accomplish it—it's unlikely that you will make the commitment to see it through. As an example, if your parents want you to be a good student, and if you view being a good student and getting good grades as something you do more for someone else rather than for yourself (as was true for Cammie), then you may not be as serious in pursuing that goal. You have to say and believe, "Meeting this goal is important to ME." So when you set a goal, own it. Write it in such a way that you believe both in the goal and in your desire to achieve it.

4. **Be sure your goal is realistic—and attainable.** There is a direct relationship between how much you believe your goal is one you can attain and your accomplishing it. For example, if you are taking a foreign-language class that requires you to memorize two hundred words for a final, and you intend to accomplish this the evening prior to the final—unless you're a real language genius, it could well be an impossible feat. But, if you break the list into a certain number of words per day per week and give yourself, say, one to two weeks to memorize them, it's more likely you'll achieve your goal.

5. **Break your goals down into manageable tasks.** Breaking a

goal into manageable tasks—and listing the activities necessary to achieve each of them—can be very helpful in accomplishing the smaller activities that lead to your bigger goal. (You'll learn more about this in the next chapter.) For example, getting into college may be one of your long-range goals, but no doubt, there are any number of things you'll need to do along the way—such as doing well in each of your classes; taking all the required entrance exams; sending for applications, filling them out and returning them; even doing things such as arranging for tuition, textbooks, room and board, and so on.

6. **Decide on the timeline for your goals.** Do you have yearly, monthly, weekly and daily goals? Like Cammie, who set her goals at the beginning of the school year, you, too, may decide to frame your goals within a school year. Or you may decide to set your goals in accordance with a calendar year, such as January 1 to December 31. Many adults use the calendar year, while many students, like Cammie, use the school year as a timeline for goal achievement. You may even opt to go month-to-month. Whatever you choose is up to you. What's important is that you give yourself a time-line to "house" your long-term and short-term goals. Thinking of your life in bigger chunks of time (such as a school term), as opposed to simply living day-to-day, will give you a better chance of meeting long-range goals. Many goals (like doing well during the school year and planning for college) require a longer period of time to accomplish. This also gives you a bigger span of time to measure your progress. If you set your timeline of goals within a school term, do so knowing precisely what month, even what week, you have targeted for completing particular tasks, all the while keeping in mind that each of these activities need to be accomplished in order to meet your larger goals.

7. **Set deadlines for completing each of your goals.** Having a

completion date helps you prioritize where and how you will allocate (spend) your time. In meeting a particular goal, if something doesn't have to be done this week or this month, you know you have time for other things. If you're nearing a deadline, you can push yourself just a little harder. Perhaps if Cammie had given herself a deadline to get each of her goals completed, she might have fared better. As an example, if she had decided on a "cut-off point" for when she would no longer wait around for Nathan Baker and his girlfriend to break up (so that he would be eligible), she might have decided to accept Lenny Stone's (or someone else's) invitation to go out. Cammie didn't meet her goal of "having a boyfriend" during her ninth-grade year, because she didn't set a deadline to give up on waiting for the breakup.

8. **Keep a copy of your goal plan in sight.** Keeping your goals where you can refer to them on a regular basis is a great way to stay focused on what's "most" important to you, even as you go about the whirlwind of your daily activities. Many teens tape their goals on their mirror, or keep them inside their day planner. Certainly this would have helped Cammie stay focused, but with nothing written down, she wasn't able to remain focused on those things she had professed were so important to her at the beginning of her school year. Consequently, Cammie failed to meet almost all of her goals.

9. **Review and revise your goals periodically.** Regardless of your timeline—be it calendar year, school term or monthly goals—review your goals periodically. Sometimes you need to add to your goals; for example, if you decide not to go to college and instead to attend a ten-month training program, you'll need to revise your plans. Or, if one of your goals is to be on a sports team and you sprain a ligament, maybe you need to revise your goal—and maybe a new

goal for getting physical therapy will need to be added. Reviewing your goals allows you to measure your progress with each of them. Cammie didn't do this, and as a result, she didn't stop the days from "slipping away from her." Perhaps if she had taken the time to review and revise her goals regularly, she would have realized that not only was time slipping away, but so were her ideals for becoming all that she had hoped to be and do during her ninth-grade year.

10. **After completing a goal, reward yourself.** You have set a goal and accomplished it. Good for you! Accomplishing a goal is a good feeling. Goal achievement is also good for your self-esteem. When you accomplish something you set out to achieve, you see yourself as capable, and you believe in your ability to be goal-oriented. You see yourself as the "winner" you are! So when you achieve a goal, celebrate! Reward yourself by doing something nice for yourself! Maybe it's a few days of just "down time"—giving yourself more time with your friends—or maybe it's a purchase, such as a new item of clothing or tickets to a special concert. Rewarding yourself is about showing appreciation (to yourself) for a "mission accomplished." If Cammie had rewarded herself after each triumph (she did meet with some success when she worked out a few times and cut down on swearing), perhaps she would have been more motivated to stay in tune with her professed goals.

VIRTUAL PRACTICE: WHAT'S YOUR READ ON "THE RULES"?

Why do you think it's important to set goals that are important to you?

_____

_____

_____

_____

_____

Has there ever been a time when it was important to achieve a particular goal, but it wasn't one you "owned"? Whose goal was it? Did you achieve the goal? Explain.

_____

_____

_____

_____

_____

Write about a time you set a goal and it wasn't realistic. What was the goal? In what way was it not realistic? How did things turn out—did you achieve it or not? What did you learn from that experience?

_____

_____

_____

_____

Do you already post your goals where you can see them? If so, have you ever had friends (or family members) make a comment about your goals? What comments did they make?

_____

_____

_____

_____

_____

Would you be embarrassed to post your goals in plain view—say, on the refrigerator, or on the mirror of your room, or on the wall next to where you study and do your homework? Explain.

_____

_____

_____

_____

_____

How do you stay organized? Do you have a calendar or a day planner? If so, how long have you used it to order and prioritize your monthly, weekly and daily goals/projects/activities? How has doing this made a difference in your life? Explain.

_____

_____

_____

_____

_____

Do any of your friends keep a day planner or use any other way of organizing their time and activities (such as a calendar where they can write in activities to complete and dates when they are due)? Explain.

_____

_____

_____

_____

_____

Do you get an allowance? If so, is it tied to specific goals, such as keeping up your share of home responsibilities? What other rewards, if any, do you receive for meeting specific goals? Do you find these rewards motivating? Explain.

_____

_____

_____

_____

_____

What sort of reward system do you think would work best to motivate you in reaching your goals? What sorts of rewards could you give yourself to celebrate your achievements?

_____

_____

_____

_____

Do you keep a log of your goals from grade to grade or year to year? How can doing that give you a sense of achievement?

_____

_____

_____

_____

It's Up to You!

Wandering aimlessly through a new town wouldn't be the most effective way to find a specific hotel, restaurant, shopping center, sports arena or whatever you were hoping to locate. Probably, you'd do better using a map, directions you'd been given or some sort of guide in finding your way around. So it is with meeting your goals. By using the goal-setting guidelines, you now have a reliable compass to guide you where you want to go.

Okay, its time for you to do some "destination" planning for yourself. So where do you want to go? Do most of your goals center around just your friends? Or are they mostly about doing well in school? Do you set goals only in times when things are getting stressful—such as when a big paper is soon due? One of the most important reasons to set goals is to keep stress at bay— and still do all of the things you want and more. Ideally, your goals should be comprehensive enough to complement *all* areas of your life.

All? That's right, and in the next chapter, you'll get a chance to check out how you can have a "full-on" life, and unlike Cammie (who felt that she lost control of her goals somewhere during the school year), how you can stay on top of all the things you want "to do, to have and to be"!

13

Nine Goals for a "Full-On" Life

Her Letter

I'll never forget the day I found the suicide letter written by my mom. I was barely eleven years old. My parents had just split up, and my mother was just beside herself with grief. (Fortunately, she decided not to kill herself.) I understood it; I was feeling incredibly sad, mixed-up and unstable myself.

I don't exactly remember too much about the next few years (I think I blocked them out of my mind as a way to cope). I do remember that I pretty much had to take care of myself. Getting myself to and from school, getting something to eat and homework—it was all up to me. It was a terrible time in so many ways. I desperately missed my father, and because things were so bitter between him and my mother, I didn't get to see him for long periods at a time. Worse, I felt for my mother, who never wanted the marriage to end—and as a result, pretty much just lost her will to live. It seemed to me that we were always moving. For four years we didn't live in the same place longer than a year. Of course, this meant that I went from one school to another—which I hated. It's awful to always have to leave your friends, and even worse to always be the "new face."

Unfortunately, there was nothing I could do about it. My mom couldn't even comfort herself, let alone her child. So I just tried to make the best of school and of the few friends I did make at each new school. It was simply the way my life was.

I'm older now, and even when I think back to those years, and most especially as I see these words on paper, I get sad all over again. The good news is, it's in the past, and I'm okay. I don't know if that is a choice I made, or an outcome of having to rely on myself. I'm not bitter. Seeing my mother so emotionally devastated made me feel sorry for her, and so, rather than be a problem to her, I became self-sufficient. I found ways to get things done. For example, if I needed to make money, I sold candy, traded video games and asked some of the adults who knew my situation if I could help them in any way—yard work, babysitting and things like that. When other kids complained about homework and making grades, I didn't have that luxury: Getting decent grades in school was really important to me, since I was hopeful that eventually it would help me get a good job and then I could get my mother the help she needed. I was worried about her, especially at times when I was our family's only means of support. There was no way I could afford not to do well in school. My future, and my mother's, depended upon it.

I'm a senior now, and my life is much different. My mother lives in Mexico, and I live in the United States with my grandparents. I'm getting a good education and know how important it is that I get a college education to be able to afford to help my mother get the help that she needs.

All in all, I'd say that while my childhood was really tough, because of it, I'm a strong person with a lot of focus. Some people tell me that I'm "wiser than my age." I like to think I am. I don't know whether that's good or bad, but it is useful. There are so many things I want—and need—to do, such as put myself through college and buy a used car, and I have only myself to rely on in making them happen. But I know I can. I don't let stress paralyze me; instead, I let it motivate me to action. I've learned to make tough decisions under pressure and that it gets easier each time. And having watched my mother get swept under by using drugs and alcohol to escape her pain, even to the point of considering suicide, I have no problems saying no to these vices.

I still remember the tears falling down my cheeks as I read my mom's suicide letter. I think that's sad that someone so young had to have that experience. But while I would never ever have chosen to endure my childhood, I believe the hardships and trials have made me a more mature and independent person. For sure, I'm stronger, and I'm emotionally stable. And I trust God to guide me through trials. It's also shaped my personality: I'm quiet, but not shy. I smile easily, but I'm not a silly person. I'm a serious person, but I have a deep appreciation for things, too. I am no one's fool. I am a doer and an achiever—which is good, because I have 101 goals!

So, while my life story seems tough, it's had a positive effect on me—the biggest of which is that I understand the importance of setting goals—because I want a "full-on" life! Having to rely on myself, and meeting my goals in the shortest amount of time possible, is something I know how to do. It has paid off for me. I see myself as getting ahead and going places. I've been accepted to a college and even secured a college scholarship. I have a good part-time job and feel really appreciated by my employer. And I feel my teachers like and support me. All this makes me a happy and grateful person.

So this is a good stage, a good time for me. I'm at peace with myself. I now look back at everything I've gone through and know it's made me more ready to take on life's challenges. I'm a successful human being! And I have much to look forward to—like achieving those 101 goals I've set for myself!

Alan Navarro, 18

What Goals Have You Set for Yourself?

Hopefully, you haven't had to face the challenges Alan has had to deal with at such an early age. It's heartening to learn that Alan has coped well with his circumstances, and in the process of realizing that he has much to do, set goals for himself to have what he so fondly refers to as a "full-on" life. Alan then goes on to point out something in which we can all take heart: Having goals for a "full-on" life means we "have much to look forward to."

What is a "full-on" life? Let's think about that. When someone asks you what your goals are, generally they ask you about something in particular. For instance, someone might ask you, "What are your career plans?" or "Have you given any thought to where you'd like to live when you're out of school?" But most likely you don't just have one key goal. If someone were to ask you what your single most important goal in life is, you'd probably have a difficult time answering the question. Maybe you would say something such as, "I want to be healthy, happy and successful," but it's such a broad statement, it seems vague and unclear.

Generally speaking, one goal doesn't cover all the things you want to "do, have and be" in your life. Alan said he had "101 goals." Do you? As you'll learn in this chapter, what's important is that you set goals in a number of areas so that you, too, can have as Alan says, a "full-on" life. After all, you have a social life, an academic life, a family life, a spiritual life, and you need time for recreation and to earn the money you need to cover those things that are your responsibility to pay for. And, of course, you'll want to explore what you'd like to do for a job or career of your choice—among other things. Accordingly, your goals should reflect a spectrum of areas, for example, plans for:

♥ Having good times and great relationships with parents, friends, teachers and others

♥ Preparing for what you'd like to do for work or career once you're out of school

♥ Your quest for spiritual meaning

♥ Satisfying your curiosity for things you would like to know more about

♥ Making money or achieving financial security or success

♥ Staying fit and healthy

♥ Having the time to pursue hobbies, sports and other interests important to you, and

♥ Gaining or maintaining respect from certain people.

VIRTUAL PRACTICE: IDENTIFYING NINE GOALS FOR YOUR "FULL-ON" LIFE

You can design goals to help assure that you have a "full-on" life. The following categories (and explanations to stimulate thinking) are useful in planning such a life. Use them to set goals that help you feel that your life is full, exciting, and that you are not missing out on all the ways that you can be using your time to fully explore your talents, hobbies and natural abilities, as well as your beliefs and quest for your meaning, purpose and achievement in life.

We asked Alan to show us his plan for accomplishing all the things he'd like to do during his school year. Here's how Alan Navarro listed his goals in each of these categories.

1. **SPIRITUAL GROWTH:** What are your goals for peace of mind, search for meaning and spiritual fulfillment?

   Goals: *I'd like to pray each day; trust God to guide me through my trials; and always thank God for all the things for which I am grateful.*

2. **PERSONAL RELATIONSHIPS:** What are your goals for

enhancing your relationships (with parents, friends, teachers, others)?

Goals: *I'd like to stay in touch with my mother, calling her whenever I can and writing her letters every week; and, to make time for my friends and tell my teachers thank-you for helping me get a good education. I'd like to find my father and get him back in my life.*

3. **LEARNING/EDUCATION:** What would you like to know more about? What skills do you want to develop?

Goals: *I'd like to stay on the honor roll.*

4. **STATUS AND RESPECT:** To which groups/organizations/ associations or affiliations do you want to belong? From whom do you want respect?

Goals: *I'd like to join the Association for Collectibles and Memorabilia—and have members think of me as someone "in the know" (which I'll do by writing a story for them about how I set up my really creative Web site).*

5. **LEISURE/HOBBIES:** What activities (hobbies, sports, travels) would you like to learn more about (or to do more of)?

Goals: *I'd like to learn how to snowboard.*

6. **FITNESS/HEALTH/WELL-BEING:** What are your goals for your physical fitness and overall health?

Goals: *I'd like to keep up my jogging at least five miles three times a week.*

7. **FINANCIAL:** What are your goals for having enough money to do the things you want to do?

   Goals: *I'd like to continue to put aside a minimum of $150 each month for college from my job at the sporting goods store; I want to send Mom $100 for her birthday in two months.*

8. **JOB/CAREER:** What kind of job would you like? What are your goals for productive work and career success?

   Goals: *Someday I'd like to run my own Web-based sports memorabilia trading company, so I want to learn all I can about sports trading cards and memorabilia, and about how to own and run a Web-based sports memorabilia trading company.*

9. **COMMUNITY SERVICE/SERVING OTHERS:** What are your plans to do "good works" within your neighborhood and community, and to help others?

   Goals: *Continue to get Mrs. Larsen's prescription from Save-on and deliver it to her at the first of the month. Check out becoming a "Big Brother."*

Reading over Alan's overall goals for his school year, you can see how they make his life look full and complete. That's one of the many benefits of creating a list of overall goals for a significant length of time, such as the school year: It gives you a design for having a life that is as full and rich as you want it to be.

In the following exercise, you'll get a chance to create goals for yourself in each of these nine categories. You'll need to set these goals within some sort of time frame. We suggest you use the timeline of a school year. In the coming chapters, you'll be using the nine goals you've created for yourself here to develop an action plan that transforms your hopes, desires, wishes and wants into a plan of action so that you can bring them to fruition.

Special note: As you do this exercise, you may be thinking about your goals overall, for example, in the job/career category. Maybe you already know what you'd like to do for work. If, like Alan, who said he wanted to own his own Web-based sports memorabilia company, you know your "final destination" or overall goal in that area, remind yourself that while you may already know the overall goal, here your intent is to identify your goal within the time frame of a school year. That way, it will be more likely that you will be able to list the activities (something you'll get to do in the next chapter) necessary for you to do this coming year to meet or further your overall goal.

In the space provided below, write down one to three goals you'd like to achieve over the next school year in each of the nine areas. Then, in the space provided to the left of each goal you've listed, rank your goals in terms of their importance to you. (Use 1 as meaning the most important and 3 being least important.) (Note: You will find a duplicate worksheet for this exercise in the Appendix. It is labeled Worksheet #1.) You'll be using this exercise again in other chapters.

1. **SPIRITUAL GROWTH:** What are your goals for peace of mind, search for meaning and spiritual fulfillment?

   ___ I'd like to: _____

   _____

   _____

   ___ I'd like to: _____

   _____

   _____

___ I'd like to: _____

_____

_____

2. **PERSONAL RELATIONSHIPS:** What are your goals for enhancing your relationships (with parents, friends, teachers, others)?

___ I'd like to: _____

_____

_____

___ I'd like to: _____

_____

_____

___ I'd like to: _____

_____

_____

3. **LEARNING/EDUCATION:** What would you like to know more about? What skills do you want to develop?

___ I'd like to: _____

_____

_____

___ I'd like to: _____

_____

_____

___ I'd like to: _____

_____

_____

4. **STATUS AND RESPECT:** To which groups/organizations/
associations or other affiliations do you want to belong?
From whom do you want respect?

___ I'd like to: _____

_____

_____

___ I'd like to: _____

_____

_____

___ I'd like to: _____

_____

_____

5. **LEISURE/HOBBIES:** What activities (hobbies, sports, travels) would you like to learn more about (or to do more of)?

___ I'd like to: _____

_____

_____

___ I'd like to: _____

_____

_____

___ I'd like to: _____

_____

_____

6. **FITNESS/HEALTH/WELL-BEING:** What are your goals for your physical fitness and overall health?

___ I'd like to: _____

_____

_____

___ I'd like to: _____

_____

_____

___ I'd like to: _____

_____

_____

7. **FINANCIAL:** What are your goals for having enough money to do the things you want to do?

___ I'd like to: _____

_____

_____

___ I'd like to: _____

_____

_____

___ I'd like to: _____

_____

_____

8. **JOB/CAREER:** What kind of job would you like? What are your goals for productive work and career success?

___ I'd like to: _____

_____

_____

___ I'd like to: _____

_____

_____

___ I'd like to: _____

_____

_____

9. **COMMUNITY SERVICE/SERVING OTHERS:** What are your plans to do "good works" within your neighborhood and community, and to help others?

___ I'd like to: _____

_____

_____

___ I'd like to: _____

_____

_____

___ I'd like to: _____

_____

_____

It's Up to You!

When you look back over the goals you listed, are you surprised that your life looks as "full-on" as it is? What did you learn? What did your goals reveal? For example, are you surprised that you had so many things you'd like to do in each of the areas? Or, in some areas, did you have a difficult time coming up with even one goal? For example, are most of your goals about being with your friends or doing well in school? Did you see any trends emerge? Did you find that many of your goals are long-range (such as getting good grades in all your classes all year) or are your goals mostly short-range (such as finding time to go shopping this weekend to buy a new pair of sneakers)? For the most part, are your goals those you can achieve in a couple of days, or do most of them require a long-range plan—such as saving up to buy a car of your own?

Either way, long-range or short-range, you can probably see that you'll be better able to achieve your goals if you break them down into manageable parts so that you can tackle them one task at a time. This next chapter will show you how to do just that.

14

Breaking Your Goals into a Manageable To-Do List

Chasing the Dragon

I really messed up my life, so now to make up for it, I've got some "Eiffel Tower plans" in place. There was a time when my biggest goal was just to get through the day—so I like to think that I've already come a long way. But to see that, you'd have to know where I've been.

Just like most kids (and like most people who end up as addicts), I didn't start out thinking I'd get hooked on drugs. I started because some of my friends smoked pot, and at the time, I didn't think it was going to change my life as drastically as it did. But once I got started, I couldn't stop. I got used to how I felt using, and it was more addictive than I'd ever imagined.

Over the next two years, my sophomore and junior years, I lost a lot of my good friends. I just got too "out of control" for them to want to hang around with me. Now I can see that as well as being in big trouble myself, I was just plain trouble to be around. At the time, I didn't care that I put a lot of strain on others. Before one good friend stopped being my friend, she said I was "too much of a drama queen," while another friend said I was "a basket case"; yet another told me, "It's too stressful being your friend." I resented them for backing away from me, but other than that, I didn't stop to think about the friendships I was losing, or the fact that I could be to blame for any of it. Instead, I saw it as their desertion and lack of loyalty—and basically said "good riddance" to their friendship.

Of course, there were other kids—a whole new "drug underworld" of them—for me to hang out with; and that's just what I did. One day, one of them offered me what he called "the ultimate high." Without thinking it through, I said, "Sure," and then I asked, "What is it?"

The guy laughed and said, "We're going to 'chase the dragon'—smoke some heroin." For a second—just a second—I was scared. I'd heard a lot about heroin, how addictive it is and how hard it is to kick. Visions of desperate, vampirelike junkies from old movies and antidrug commercials came to my mind. But I tried it anyway. After all, I reasoned, we were just going to smoke it. There'd be no needles involved. So I did—even though it made me sick to my stomach and made me feel bad about myself. It was powerfully addictive. I could only stay high for so long, and then I needed more. Of course, the guy who "turned me on" to heroin the first time didn't want to give me free drugs every day—but I needed more and more of the drug every day. So then I started stealing things to trade for getting it. It was a terrible thing. I was making myself feel like the biggest loser in the entire world for using, and worse, because I was using all the time, I was building up an even greater tolerance for needing it. In short, I had become chemically dependent: I was a full-blown addict.

Meanwhile, my grades, my weight and my overall appearance all plummeted to unimaginable depths. When I started drinking and smoking pot, I got pretty comfortable with lying. It's not like you can tell your parents the truth about what you're doing and where you're going if you're going out to get high. So I wasn't the most honest person around to begin with, but when I started "chasing the dragon" I lied about everything I was doing, where my money went, why I kept needing more money, and where everything I owned of any value was going. And, of course, I was stealing to support my habit.

I've never felt more trapped and miserable in my whole life. I had to go make that money every day, or else I'd get sick—and I mean physically sick, to say nothing of this awful craving I'd have in my head that wouldn't leave me alone. It was like I was living to use and using to live.

One day I was caught shoplifting. My parents came to the jail to bail me out. Luckily for me, they knew more was going on than my being rebellious and deciding to become a thief. I say that because it was the beginning of a turnaround for me. I was so miserable that when my parents began questioning me, I broke down and told them I was using drugs. My parents took me to a counselor, who referred me to an inpatient drug and alcohol treatment program. I went through withdrawals and got really sick (even though I "just smoked it"). My nose ran, my skin crawled; my muscles and even my bones ached. I was so sick to my stomach that I couldn't eat anything for four days, and I couldn't sleep at all for five days.

I never want to go through that again. I learned at the treatment center that addiction is what they call "a progressive disease," which means it would only be worse the next time. What I went through was bad enough!

Kicking my drug habit was the hardest thing I have ever done. My counselor at the treatment center told me it would take real courage to stay clean. Boy, was that ever the truth.

So if you're using, my heart feels for you, because there's nothing good that can come from it. My advice would be for you to stop using and get the help you need before your life ends up being even more of a hell than it already is. The first step is admitting you have a problem and making a decision to reach out to get the help you need. That was the first goal in my recovery, and it remains my most important goal on a daily basis.

It's been two years now since I've taken any kind of drug or alcohol. I still go to Twelve-Step meetings on a regular basis. My life has gotten so much better. Since I've been clean, I've set and met a lot of goals—in every area of my life—and I continue setting them. I had to change just about everything. I set goals in rebuilding my relationship with my parents and goals in making new "clean and sober" friends. I also needed to set goals to have fun that didn't involve alcohol or drugs. My first year clean, it was a real accomplishment for me to meet my goal of going to a school dance and dancing while completely sober. Since then I've gone to theme parks with the school, camping with my friend and her family, belly-boarding at the beach—all the kinds of things I would've thought were just too "uncool" to try before—and I had a lot of fun, which was the goal. My next goal is to take up flying stunt-kites. A guy I'm dating says it is so much fun that we have to try it—and I'm really looking forward to it.

I'm still meeting and working toward some major goals when it comes to education. I really fell behind in the years I was using drugs. I've made a lot of progress, but I still have more goals to meet in that area if I'm going to graduate this June (a year after my class), but I've brought up my grade point average each semester. I then want to go to college and become a certified substance abuse counselor. When it comes to a career goal, I'm really clear: I want to work as a substance abuse counselor at a recovery home for women. I've made it my goal to at least get my internship at this great program in town that works with women who are out of detox and inpatient treatment, and working on building a foundation for their recovery in the community before living on their own. That sounds like the most awesome career in the world to me: being able to help other women grow strong in their recovery and learn more about themselves. So that's my goal—to shape a career around what I've learned. But, like I said, my most important goal is always to stay free of drugs, because I know I can't reach any of my other goals unless I succeed at that one.

Jordanne Guy, 19

Goals, Like Destinations, Are Reached One Step at a Time

Some goals, such as to become a scientist or to have a wonderful family (or, as in the story above, to become a substance abuse counselor), are big, bold and ambitious—or, as Jordanne said, "Eiffel Tower plans." Many times, the accomplishment of goals, especially those that are broad and long-range, requires that you take lots of steps in between in order to move you toward your bigger goal. Certainly this is true for plans for the future, such as going to college—which means that you'll want to do things such as get good grades year by year in order to meet your overall goal of getting accepted into a college of your choice.

Perhaps when you look over the goals you listed in the last chapter, you can see how much easier they appear to be attained when they're broken down into manageable tasks.

We asked Jordanne to select one of her goals and then to list all of the necessary things she would have to do in meeting this specific goal. She selected her #1 goal in the Career/Job category: *I want to be a substance abuse counselor for women in a recovery program,* and listed the activities necessary to meeting this goal:

♥ Stay free of drugs.
♥ See my school's guidance counselor to learn what the requirements are for getting into college.
♥ See my guidance counselor to learn what the requirements

are for getting a degree and for completing requirements to be certified as a substance abuse counselor.

♥ Research and apply to colleges in the area.

♥ Get on the Internet to research available grants and scholarships.

♥ Check on the requirements for becoming a counselor at a recovery home for women.

♥ Make appointments with people who are doing the job I want to be doing (starting with my former counselor), so I can interview them to see what kind of advice they can offer me for getting into the field.

♥ Check on an internship at this great program in town that works with women who are working on building a foundation for their recovery before living on their own.

♥ Just to make sure I don't limit my options, visit at least four other local inpatient treatment programs, to see how their programs work and what they have to offer in the form of internship training.

♥ Apply for volunteer work at a treatment program over the summer, so I can have my foot in the door when the time comes to get an internship.

As you can see, Jordanne has a lot to do! (And no doubt you will, too.) Listing all the steps necessary to accomplish a goal is important: It helps you decide the best time and the best strategy for individually tackling each necessary task. (In the next few chapters, you'll get a chance to see how these tasks can be assigned to a monthly, weekly and daily plan so that you can reach your goal.)

VIRTUAL PRACTICE: WHAT DO YOU NEED TO DO TO ACHIEVE YOUR GOALS?

To begin, refer back to the last chapter and then use the space identified in this exercise to list only your #1 goal in each of the nine categories. Next, list all of the tasks you will have to complete in order to reach that goal, as well as the month in which each task must be accomplished. (Note: We have only provided space for you to list activities for your #1 goal in each area. In the Appendix at the back of this book, you will find a duplicate worksheet you can use or copy for your other goals in each category. It is labeled Worksheet #2.)

1. **SPIRITUAL GROWTH**
My #1 Goal: _____

_____

_____

Tasks to do in meeting this goal: **Must be completed by:**

_____

_____

_____

_____

_____

_____

_____

_____

2. PERSONAL RELATIONSHIPS
My #1 Goal: _____

_____

_____

Tasks to do in meeting this goal: **Must be completed by:**

_____

_____

_____

_____

_____

_____

_____

_____

3. LEARNING/EDUCATION
My #1 Goal: _____

_____

_____

Tasks to do in meeting this goal: **Must be completed by:**

_____

_____

_____

_____

_____

_____

4. STATUS AND RESPECT
My #1 Goal: _____

_____

_____

Tasks to do in meeting this goal: **Must be completed by:**

_____

_____

_____

_____

_____

_____

_____

5. LEISURE/HOBBIES
My #1 Goal: _____

_____

_____

Tasks to do in meeting this goal: **Must be completed by:**

_____

_____

_____

_____

_____

_____

6. FITNESS/HEALTH/WELL-BEING
My #1 Goal: _____

_____

_____

Tasks to do in meeting this goal: **Must be completed by:**

_____

_____

_____

_____

_____

_____

_____

_____

7. FINANCIAL
My #1 Goal: _____

_____

_____

Tasks to do in meeting this goal: **Must be completed by:**

_____

_____

_____

_____

_____

_____

8. JOB/CAREER
My #1 Goal: _____

_____

_____

Tasks to do in meeting this goal: **Must be completed by:**

_____

_____

_____

_____

_____

_____

_____

9. COMMUNITY SERVICE/SERVING OTHERS
My #1 Goal: _____

_____

_____

Tasks to do in meeting this goal: **Must be completed by:**

_____

_____

_____

_____

_____

_____

_____

Now take a few minutes to review your goals and the tasks required to accomplish them. You can feel a sense of satisfaction knowing that you've actually moved closer to realizing those goals just by breaking them down into a list of achievable tasks! Setting a deadline for each of those tasks is also sure to keep you moving forward on the road to reaching your goals—and possibly alert you if you've veered off-course.

It's Up to You!

You've made real progress generating overall goals in the nine different categories, and now having listed the activities necessary to accomplish those goals. But you know that the mere setting of goals doesn't necessarily mean you'll get them accomplished.

So why isn't a list of goals enough? Because you have a million-and-one things to do, many of which crop up on a day-by-day basis—not to mention an occasional crisis here and there. Besides, especially now that you've set goals for a full-on life, you'll need to manage your time wisely. Breaking your activities into a monthly to-do list is the key to good time (and goal) management.

The next chapter will show you how to manage your overall goals by creating a monthly to-do list.

15

Breaking Your Goals into Monthly "To-Do's"

On the Roster . . . of the USA National Team

In sixth grade, I always watched the athletes and wished I could be like them. I started playing volleyball on a team, which was really a joke back then . . . something that a bunch of us did for fun after school. We had two games and lost pitifully both times. I wasn't an athlete, and I had no idea what serious volleyball was, until three years ago.

In seventh grade, I decided to start playing club volleyball. I progressed slightly at the game during this club season, but by the end of an awful eighth-grade school season, I knew I wanted to get better and to play this game at a serious competitive level. While I did make the top team for my age range, I was very aware that my skill didn't even compare to some of the other girls on the team. But I wanted to be the best, so I practiced, and played my hardest. By the middle of the season, I was much better: I was a starter and was one of the lead scorers for my team. But still, I felt I hadn't developed the "mentally tough" attitude that I needed to be the very best of the best—until my freshman year. That year, a team I played on placed seventeenth at the national competition in Salt Lake City.

Toward the end of the season, I decided I wanted to try out for the USA Volleyball High Performance Camp. This camp is available only to girls who qualify as the top thirty players in the country. Each year nearly fifteen hundred players vie for one of these coveted spots, so you can imagine how thrilled I was when I learned that I'd been selected to attend the camp. It was held in Colorado Springs that summer, and while there, I had the privilege of seeing Logan Tomm and the USA National Team play. (Logan Tomm is considered the number-one best player on the USA National Volleyball Team and a starter on the number-one team in the nation—Stanford.) Watching the USA National Team play was so exciting. And it was the start of a dream for me, a dream that has become a goal. As I watched the USA National Team play, I saw and felt an "intensity" and love for the game— like playing was a "celebration" for each player. It was such a joyous and powerful thing to witness, to see and feel. Watching that game, I knew then and there, I wanted to play on the USA National Team. I vowed I'd do what it takes to one day be on the team.

I'm sure I was a "different" player when I returned to my own team. Having set the goal to one day play on the USA National Team meant that every move I made was a deliberate attempt to play my best at all times. In addition to knowing that I needed to give my all in every game, I returned knowing that while the game was about my best, it was also about "team" best. So that next year when I played varsity for my school again, I played knowing that my skills had to coincide with each member of the team. So I played each game with a "think team" approach, and that's when I discovered the real meaning of being "mentally tough." In the middle of our season, we even beat a team that we'd never been able to beat before, and I know it's because we were now learning to think and act as a team. We had all learned to put into practice a term our coach had used so often: "team mentality." The results were good: We finished second in Southern California and third in the state.

I know I have a really long way to go to reach my goal of being on the USA National Team, but I know I can and will do it. Every day counts, so I'm driven by my goal, even on those days when I wake up and say, "Ugh, I don't want to weight lift and train today! I don't want to go to practice today." When I feel this way, I remind myself of my goal and then say, "C'mon, Emily, if you're going to play on the USA National Team, you've got to do this." That voice is very convincing. It reassures me of my commitment to meet my goal—and reminds me how much time and work I've already put into meeting it. So I get up and go, because one day soon, when the roster of members is announced for those who made the USA National Team, my name will posted.

Emily Robinson, 15

Do You Create a Monthly To-Do List?

Emily's story shows us how she's made progress each year, moving closer and closer to her goal of being on the national volleyball team. She started out not being an athlete in the sixth grade, yet was selected to go to High Performance Camp following her freshman year in high school. That's progress!

Emily has set a steady course of goals that need to be met on a monthly basis in order to move her toward reaching her big dream, and Emily has continued to succeed! She's done this while keeping up her grades, making time for family and friends, and regularly attending Youth Rallies and other youth functions at her church.

No doubt you also have a rigorous schedule. Most teens lead active and busy lives: There's the workload of six or seven high-school courses, extracurricular activities, time with family and friends, and daily responsibilities at home—cleaning your room, doing laundry, helping with meal preparation and caring for the family pet, to name a few. All are activities that must get done on a regular basis. And then, in addition, there are your dreams for achieving some very important goals for your life right now, and for your plans for the future. How do you manage it all? The answer: You prioritize your larger, overall goals into monthly activities (and then, into weekly and daily to-do's—but more on this later).

Listing what needs to be done and when it needs to be completed will help you get things done without feeling overwhelmed or as if you aren't covering all the bases.

In looking over your lists of activities in the last chapter, are you able to see that while some of these to-do's need to be done soon, like within the coming weeks, others could be put off—like for weeks or even months? That's the benefit of listing the activities necessary to meeting your overall goals on a monthly basis; it allows you to see "at a glance" what needs to be done—in that time frame so you can focus on that and not worry about the rest. Prioritizing your activities helps you stay organized and in charge of your time.

To illustrate the simplicity and benefits of organizing your activities, we asked Emily to list all the things she needed to do to meet her #1 goal in all of the nine categories for the month of March.

Here's her list for that month:

March To-Do's	Must be completed by:
Attend the Youth Rally at my church	3/31
Get Mom's birthday gift	3/10
Plan trip to New Jersey to see Nicole	start now!
Find out dates for USA Youth Team tryouts	3/5

March To-Do's	Must be completed by:
Start reading the Bible more	start now
Get Sammi Incubus CD	3/10
Start communicating with colleges I'm interested in attending	start now
Read at least one of the new books I've bought	3/30
Increase vertical jump	start now
Work on endurance (run for thirty minutes straight at least three times a week)	ongoing
Start saving up to buy camera	spring break
Decide if Geoff or Brody is best date for the prom	3/30
A on English essay	3/22
Ask my coach to write a letter of recommendation for my college files	3/15
Bring my speed and stamina up— running seven miles four days a week	3/30
Work sixteen hours at my part-time job	ongoing
Turn in this year's volleyball camp application	3/15

VIRTUAL PRACTICE: CREATING YOUR MONTHLY TO-DO LIST

Okay, it's your turn to apply this skill. In the last chapter, you created a list of activities for each of your #1 goals in the nine categories. Using the worksheet space provided in this section, categorize the activities from each of your #1 goals according to what

needs to be done month-by-month. (You'll find a duplicate of this
worksheet in the Appendix. It is labeled Worksheet #3. You can
use it to work through your goals #2 and #3 in each of the nine
categories.) Don't forget, in the space to the right of the list you're
creating, jot down the date each task needs to be completed.
Note: We've used the January to December calendar here, so if
you use September to August, just label it accordingly.

January To-Do's   **Must be completed by:**

_____

_____

_____

_____

_____

_____

_____

_____

_____

_____

_____

_____

February To-Do's   **Must be completed by:**

_____

_____

_____

_____

_____

_____

_____

_____

_____

_____

_____

March To-Do's   **Must be completed by:**

_____

_____

_____

_____

_____

_____

_____

_____

_____

_____

_____

April To-Do's   **Must be completed by:**

_____

_____

_____

_____

_____

_____

_____

_____

_____

_____

_____

May To-Do's   **Must be completed by:**

_____

_____

_____

_____

_____

_____

_____

_____

_____

_____

_____

June To-Do's   **Must be completed by:**

_____

_____

_____

_____

_____

_____

_____

_____

_____

_____

July To-Do's   **Must be completed by:**

_____

_____

_____

_____

_____

_____

_____

_____

_____

_____

August To-Do's   **Must be completed by:**

_____

_____

_____

_____

_____

_____

_____

_____

_____

_____

_____

September To-Do's   **Must be completed by:**

_____

_____

_____

_____

_____

_____

_____

_____

_____

_____

_____

October To-Do's   **Must be completed by:**

_____

_____

_____

_____

_____

_____

_____

_____

_____

_____

November To-Do's   **Must be completed by:**

_____

_____

_____

_____

_____

_____

_____

_____

_____

_____

December To-Do's   **Must be completed by:**

_____

_____

_____

_____

_____

_____

_____

_____

_____

_____

_____

_____

It's Up to You!

Again, we encourage you to set goals in each of the nine categories. In the beginning, if this seems a little overwhelming, you can begin with two or three areas. Then, when you can see how easy this method of breaking your goals into manageable parts is, you can add on until you have developed goals in all nine categories. Whether you set one goal or many, be sure to break your goals into the activities you want to accomplish for a particular month.

Even looking over a list of monthly to-do's can seem daunting—but don't let it stop you from believing you can do it! The important thing is not to get overwhelmed; it won't take you long to become an "expert" at setting goals. Now that you have your to-do's for the months ahead of you, the next step is to create a list of weekly and daily to-do's that coincide with your monthly ones. Our next chapter will show you the importance of breaking your monthly goals into weekly to-do's, as well as how to do this.

16

Breaking Your Monthly Goals into Weekly "To-Do's"

My Goal Is to Be Very Rich!

My goal is to be really rich. I think this is a very important goal and a very worthwhile one. I've also thought that it would be great to earn enough money to have a really nice lifestyle—which my mother defines as being able to have your family live in a safe neighborhood and attend good schools—and my father defines as being able to take the whole family on vacation without a "shoestring budget" to live on while vacationing. (He also says it means that he'd retire early, join a golf club and play golf every day.) My idea of being rich is to have thousands and thousands and thousands of dollars. And maybe a few thousand more! I want to be rich so that I can have a great lifestyle—which is, as my parents say, the main reason to make money in the first place. And, of course, I'd buy all the things I need and want—which right now includes a new car. But the biggest reason for my wanting to be rich is so that I can be a philanthropist.

I've always admired those who look around, see a worthy cause and write a check with the flick of a pen; they are able to make something awesome happen. Every time I hear of someone in need—a poor family needing assistance, a child or senior citizen needing medical care, a center that faces closing its doors if the agency or organization can't raise adequate funding (like a center for the homeless in my town)—I always think how cool it would be if I could write a check to help out. Thinking of all the good things I could do if only I had the money makes me want to be rich—really rich!

Because I feel it would be just great to be able to help those in need, or as my Uncle Angus calls it, to "redistribute wealth," I especially tune in when I hear of others who are doing just that. I especially admire Joan Kroc (think McDonald's). She's a great humanitarian and generous philanthropist.

I've even thought about how I'd like to go about giving my money away. I think I'd "redistribute" my wealth in the manner that Joan Kroc chooses to do. Mrs. Kroc gives money to worthy causes such as women's shelters, children's hospitals, even a Peace Process Center at a major university. Most people don't even know a lot of the things she supports and funds because she wants it that way. A couple of years ago, when North Dakota had an incredible flood that left practically one whole town without housing, I remember hearing that a "silent angel" had donated a huge amount of money for those whose homes and possessions had been swept away. When I read about it, I cried, thinking how awesome it was that someone would want to help out others—without any acclaim for themselves. Of course the whole country tried and tried to find out who the "silent angel" could be, and it wasn't until months later that someone traced the good deed back to Joan Kroc.

I just think helping others is the best thing for the human heart. Now, I'm not saying that only the rich should give, or that if your donation to others is a small gift that it's not important—because it is. I'm just saying that why not be able to make a contribution that helps large numbers of people—and to do it all the time!

The idea of being able to give all the time really hit home for me in the aftermath of the September 11 terrorist attack on America. When so many people lost loved ones, and needed both emergency and long-term relief, the Red Cross stepped in with fund-raising efforts and raised millions of dollars. And you know what, while the money helped, it was only a drop in the bucket in terms of how much more was needed. And then, watching the images of so many homeless people who endured starvation in Afghanistan—and knowing these conditions are faced by so many people around the world—well, having money to help out can be a good thing.

I think that anyone can make money and save money (and give it to others) if they choose that as a goal. I read an article about a little old lady named Oseola McCarty, who was a retired washerwoman. She spent seventy-five years of her life doing housekeeping and laundry for others. She lived a simple life, so simple that most people who knew her believed she was destitute. But Oseola saved up $250,000! Then, she gave $150,000 to the University of Southern Mississippi for scholarships for students who wouldn't be able to go to school otherwise. And to think she only had a sixth-grade education! I'd say she was one smart lady! Of course, everyone was amazed and impressed by her selfless generosity. Not only does her story really inspire me, it also shows me that you can achieve almost any goal if you're truly dedicated to it—especially one that's as worthy as being able to give to others. And that's my goal. I want to be rich. I figure if I can just chip away at my goals week by week, I can meet my goal of being able to "redistribute" my wealth.

Tyanna Leigh Dayton, 17

Do You Have a Weekly To-Do List?

Tyanna Leigh didn't tell us of her plans for becoming "very rich" (nor what her bank balance is right now), but chances are, she's going to have to put some serious goals in place. But all goals, especially those as aggressive as "being very rich," need a carefully laid plan to bring them to fruition. Like most goals, Tyanna Leigh's list of activities in meeting her overall goals will be lengthy, and she'll have to stick to a "plan" if she wants to join the ranks of philanthropists such as the Joan Krocs of the world.

She is well aware of it. "I used to think that summers went by all too fast," Tyanna Leigh told us, "but so does a semester—and so can a month. When a new Rad Rags store opened and I saw that they were hiring part-time cashiers, I knew that was the job I wanted. Their clothes are so cool. My cousin worked for their store in her hometown and she got all sorts of beautiful clothes at these unbelievable employee-discount prices. Plus, all the popular girls shop there, so you have an 'in' with them. It was the perfect job for me. The first week they were taking applications, I had a huge report to write, and it seemed to take up every minute I wasn't in school or doing something majorly important with friends. The next week, I spent all this time I should've spent the previous week on practicing for tryouts on the tennis team, which was the following week. Then my jacket needed to go to the drycleaners, and my parents said if I didn't wash the car I couldn't use it the following week. The following week the actual tennis team tryouts occurred, preceded by days of frantic shopping for the perfect tennis outfit to wear for try-outs. In the middle of all three of these weeks, there was always more homework and studying for three tests. The fourth week, not only was there practice with the tennis team (I made the team), but Steve Reid had finally called the previous weekend and asked me to meet him at the mall so we could 'talk,' which was the sign of interest I'd been waiting for all school year. After that, I had to make time for his calls and meeting him after school and during lunch. By the time I got to Rad Rags to apply, the month was over, the sign was down and they weren't hiring anymore."

How about you? Do you, like Tyanna Leigh, start the month with great intentions of getting specific things accomplished and then suddenly the month is over and some goals remain—still a goal but unaccomplished? That's the importance of making a list of what needs to be done for the month at hand, and then breaking these activities into what needs to be done on a weekly basis. (In the next chapter, you'll see the simplicity and importance of breaking them down into daily goals, but for now, let's concentrate on turning monthly goals into weekly to-do's.)

We asked Tyanna Leigh to share with us her goals for the month at hand. She listed them as:

Monthly To-Do's	Must be completed by:
Go to church 4x	4x
Throw B-day party for Sienna	2/10
Complete history project	2/28
Excel on the cheerleading squad	2/28
Make at least $75	2/28
Go to Valentine's Day dance	2/17
Work out 12x	2/28
Expand my baby-sitting business	2/21

Now, let's take a look at Tyanna Leigh's goals for the month, broken into weekly activities.

Goals for Week #1

1. *Call the four families I baby-sit for, and let them know I'm available and "looking for work"*
2. *Cheerleading practice*

3. Call Grams and ask her for money for my B-day instead of some other gift
4. Regular Saturday baby-sitting job for Kitty and Billy Thornton from 2–5 ($10)
5. Talk to Brittany about having a B-day party for Sienna
6. Make invitations to Sienna's B-day party
7. Get to school early: Kevin has band practice—hang out with Brit near band room
8. Work out three times
9. Ask Kendra Jacobs for a ride home from cheerleading practice next week (Mom working late). Need to start my big paper!
10. Check out library reference books for history project
11. Go to church
12. Ask Brit if she'll hand off my letter to Kevin asking if he's going to the school dance on Friday (Spray the note w/perfume just before I leave the house.)

Goals for Week #2

1. Regular Saturday baby-sitting job for Kitty and Billy Thornton from 2–5 ($10)
2. Call the Hansons and the Whites on baby-sitting jobs
3. Follow up on phone calls to potential baby-sitting jobs
4. Throw Sienna's party on Saturday (order cake/pizza/ collect money for soft drinks)
5. Ask my brother to trade Thursday (my night/computer) for Tuesday (his night/computer) to complete history project
6. Turn in history project

7. Work out three times
8. Cheerleading practice
9. Secure date for Valentine's Day dance (hopefully with Kevin)
10. Go to church

Goals for Week #3

1. Regular Saturday baby-sitting job for Kitty and Billy Thornton from 2–5 ($10)
2. Call Mrs. Moreno and Mrs. Samuels about upcoming baby-sitting jobs
3. Report cards are out next week. Since I know I have at least 2 A's, 2 B's and 3 C's, ask my parents if they are willing to reward A's with $15, B's with $10, and C's with $5. If my grades are as I expect them to be, that would be $65 right there!
4. Work out three times
5. Cheerleading practice
6. Call Grandma/check on whether she sent money!
7. Get my hair trimmed after school for the dance
8. Talk to Robin about what she's wearing to the dance
9. Go to Valentine's Day dance (hopefully with Kevin)
10. Go to church

Goals for Week #4

1. Regular Saturday baby-sitting job for Kitty and Billy Thornton from 2–5 ($10)
2. Collect!!!$$$!!!! from my parents for my good grades! Yesssssss!

3. *Follow up on phone calls to potential baby-sitting jobs*
4. *Work out three times*
5. *Cheerleading practice*
6. *Cheerleading/game against East High*
   Practice: Bring my best tennis shoes
7. *Go to the mall with Robin (check out Nordy's!)*
8. *Go to movies w/Brit*
9. *Baby-sit for Brian Tulley, 4–5:30 on Sunday (earn $5)*
10. *Go to church*

VIRTUAL PRACTICE: CREATING YOUR WEEKLY TO-DO LISTS

Now it's time for you to develop your weekly to-do lists. Using the monthly activities you identified in the last chapter, write what you will need to do on a weekly basis throughout this coming month in order to reach your overall goals. (Note: You will find an additional copy of this worksheet in the Appendix. It is labeled Worksheet #4.)

Goals for Week #1

_____

_____

_____

_____

_____

_____

_____

_____

_____

_____

_____

_____

Goals for Week #2

_____

_____

_____

_____

_____

_____

_____

_____

_____

_____

Goals for Week #3

_____

_____

_____

_____

_____

_____

_____

_____

_____

_____

Goals for Week #4

_____

_____

_____

_____

_____

_____

_____

_____

_____

_____

It's Up to You!

Making—and accomplishing—a weekly to-do list can help you stay on track toward meeting your goals. As you check off those things you've accomplished, and check to see what's coming up, you are able to see how you're spending your time in a balanced, worthwhile way. A sense of accomplishment is always a good feeling, and one that contributes to your feeling positive about yourself—in other words, you gain a reputation with yourself as a doer, an achiever and someone who is taking charge of his or her life. The result is sure to be healthy self-esteem.

So now on to the next step: breaking your weekly tasks into daily to-do's. This next chapter will show you why it's valuable for you to do this and just how to go about getting it done.

17

Creating Your Daily To-Do Lists

My Snake Is Missing: Have You Seen It?

A couple of weeks back, my family and I were staying at a cabin in the mountains. One day I saw a sleek and really beautiful four-foot gopher snake. The snake noticed me and, rather than hurrying away, edged a little closer, like it was curious about me. I stood there talking to it and, sure enough, the snake did want to make my acquaintance! Being rather friendly, it slithered my way, close enough for the two of us to get a really good look at each other. I leaned down, picked it up, and within moments, the gorgeous creature wrapped her pretty self around my arm. I swear that snake purred while it enjoyed the warmth of my skin. I told her I'd sure like to take her home with me, and I thought she smiled at me—like she was pleading with me to let her live in an aquarium in my house. "Done deal!" I assured her. "You are now my pet."

Of course, I asked Dad if I could take it home first. He said, and I quote, "As long as you are a responsible pet owner." I swore I would be. But heck, I wanted that snake and would promise anything to have her. Are you with me on this?

I put my new pet in a paper sack with vent holes so she'd have air, placed her in the trunk for her ride to her new home, and off we went. Well, having been a pet owner for all of two hours, how was I to remember there was a snake in our trunk? So our family reached home, and everyone was unpacking the car. I opened the trunk and started taking out things, when suddenly two red reptilian eyes lurched at me. The next thing I heard was the thud of my back hitting the pavement, and I lay gasping for air. I mean, I've never been so scared in all my life. Scrambling to my feet, I yelled, *"I'll* unpack the trunk!" I quickly got everything out, looking for the snake as I did. It was nowhere to be found. So, thinking it needed a little time to calm down—like I did—I closed the trunk and went to the fridge to get something to eat and have time to regroup from my panic attack. About twenty minutes later, I returned to search for my new pet.

I looked and looked, but simply couldn't find that reptile. I decided it needed more time to come out of its hiding place. Several hours later when everyone was unpacked and our family was buzzing with the normal activities of home, Dad asked, "How's that snake adjusting, Son? Did you get her all set up in the aquarium?"

"Well, Dad," I told him (I mean, he was coming down the hall to my room, and I'd neither set up the aquarium nor located my snake, so it wasn't like I didn't have to level with him about my snake being missing), "just one small problem. She's still sleeping in the car, so I didn't want to disturb her."

"She's where?" he yelled. "Let's get that &*!#% snake out of my car, NOW!"

"Sure thing, Dad!" I said, following my dad who was nearly on a run to the garage. We couldn't find the snake. We even took out the mat, the spare tire and all the tire tools. So then, thinking the snake had found a hole and crawled into the back seat of the car, we searched the back seat, too. We looked everywhere including under the seats, and then in and around the front seats. That snake wasn't in any of these places. "I'll get a flashlight," my dad barked and strode into the house to get one. The next sounds I heard was my sister screaming and my dad consoling my mother. "No, the snake can't be on the loose in the house, it's still somewhere in the car—or the garage." My dad returned with the flashlight and searched the entire car again. And then, stretched out across the entire front seat, he searched under the dashboard—where he discovered the snake, coiled around all those cute colored wires, and in none-too-good of a snake mood either. The minute the beam from Dad's flashlight hit that snake's eyes, it HISSSSSED loud enough, it seemed, for the neighbors to hear. Frightened out of his wits, my dad let out a blood-curdling yell and rolled out of the car so fast you wouldn't believe it.

"He's on the wires," my dad said and then barked, "Get that #@!*# snake out of my car!" Guess he wasn't wild about a snake being within millimeters of his femoral artery. Believing the snake was just minutes away from my putting her in the aquarium, my dad left the scene. But here's the thing: While my dad and I were having our panic attack, the snake had slithered off to a new hiding place. I searched every last inch of the car and the garage, but the snake had vanished into thin air. Luckily, and surprisingly, no one in my family asked me about the snake that night. What a relief that was! Maybe it was because on my way to my room that evening, I announced, "Good night, everybody! I've got a huge test tomorrow and need to hit the books!" Having said that, I closed the door to my room and didn't come out again.

I did my homework and went to bed, but I didn't get much sleep that night. I kept thinking about the moment when the light hit that snake's eyes, and they lit up as it hissed. It was such a "dangerous" sound. So around midnight, I got up to search for the snake, but once again, no luck. So I went back to bed, deciding that I'd get up really early the next day to check for the snake—but it never happened. Still tired, I got up later than I'd planned and, running late, I barely got myself together for school, let alone to have time to go search for the snake. When my mom called, "I'm leaving—anyone not in the car in the next two minutes doesn't get a ride to school," I grabbed my books and headed for the car—praying that the snake was still in there, but that no one would sit on it or discover it in any way.

I'd promised myself that the moment school let out, I'd head straight for home and search for the snake in the garage. But my friends all suggested we go get smoothies at our favorite place at a nearby mall, so I totally forgot about my plans to find the snake. Next we played some pool, one thing led to another and by the time I got home, I'd completely forgotten until I saw everyone in my family. They looked so "comfy" and content that I didn't have the heart to let them know the snake was still on the loose. So I just let it go for the night, once again promising myself that I'd find that snake first thing the next morning—or after school, one of the two. But on Tuesday, I woke up late and had to dash off, and after school I had football practice. Then my friend Kevin asked me to go help him pick out a new CD. By the time I got home, my parents were camped out in the living room watching television, and my sister was in the kitchen trying to make cupcakes for a classmate's birthday party at school the next day. So it really wasn't possible to go rummaging through the car without letting on that it was because I hadn't yet found the snake.

On Wednesday I went to watch Lexi Johnson try out for a part in a play. She asked me to be there and, well, I've been crazy about Lexi all year and once she asked me to be there, nothing else entered my mind—including the missing reptile. By Thursday, I wasn't even thinking "snake"—I mean, it's not like she'd become a member of the family or anything. Nor had I grown attached to her: I hadn't seen her for days! So one thing having led to another, Saturday arrived before I remembered: The snake was still on the loose—either in some remote location in the family car, or slithering around in the garage—or maybe it had escaped the garage and had crawled back to the mountain by now. Maybe it had even starved to death!

My pet snake has been missing for six days, and I didn't have the nerve to tell anyone in the house. I mean, if my mother knew, she'd put the house up for sale! That is, if she managed to live through the horror of it. And I don't even want to consider the consequences from my dad: The car, the free gas, all the privileges I've earned to spend time with my friends on weekends— all would be taken away for who knows how long. As for my sister, she would faint dead away—along with her little friends (who I swear live at our house more than their own). So, I can't let on that the snake is missing—though it can't be much longer until Dad comes into my room to look at the snake. I don't have to worry about my sister or my mom. Both are terrified of snakes and have no desire to pay a visit to my room—where it isn't, at least not yet. But I'm so afraid that one of them is going to find that snake while in the garage (because that's where I assume it's hiding out.) So of course, I have to find the snake before the snake finds someone else, and one of my family members dies of a heart attack when they're greeted by a surprise run-in with the snake. And I really don't want the poor thing to die from not having had a meal in over a week.

So, bottom line is that finding that snake is something I absolutely have to do! I just keep forgetting—or something else comes up that seems more urgent (at least at the time). I've seen notes my mom leaves to herself around the house, lists of reminders: "Pick up dry cleaning . . . Call dentist to schedule kids' checkups . . . Buy trash bags . . . PTA meeting at 6:00 . . ." While I always jot down my goals for the week, with all the trouble I seem to be having with getting around to my snake-hunt, I wonder if I need a daily reminder, something that says, "Urgent: Find snake TODAY!"

Colin Sinclair, 18

Do You Make a Daily To-Do List?

Does it sound to you as if it's a wise decision for Colin to make a to-do list with "find my snake—today!" at the very top of it? We think so—and we're hoping he did find the snake before his family did—or before it died from starvation!

How about you? Do you start your week promising yourself you're going to get so much accomplished but then, well, life happens (as Colin found out) and before you know it, the week is over and you didn't accomplish all you'd hoped? It can happen. Does it happen to you?

Do you find that you start the week with great intentions, but then get sidetracked with a million-and-one things to do? That's the importance of a daily to-do list. It gives you the list of things you must get done today right there in black and white—bar none. While you may put the usual things on your list, such as classes or regularly scheduled sports practice or any extra-curricular activities you attend, your daily to-do list should also include those things to get done from the goals you created within nine key categories.

To create your daily to-do list, begin by reviewing your goals for the week at hand. Most teens do this on the weekend, such as when they're doing homework. Then at the start of each day—or the prior evening—they review their goals for the upcoming day so they are prepared for what greets them. This way, they know what they need to do to stay on course for the day. This is really helpful because it allows you to gather up the necessary books or get permission slips signed by your parents and so on, so you can be as "on top of things" as possible. With your sights clearly set, you can then create a daily to-do list accordingly.

Colin, like most teens, has a busy schedule that includes doing well in his classes, working at his part-time job, and spending time with his family and friends as well as with his girlfriend. He's also on the football team, which meets for regular practices.

All of those things should be reflected on his daily to-do list. But as you know from reading his story, Colin's weekly goals also need to reflect the "emergency" he's having—which means locating the snake he brought from the mountains hoping to house in an aquarium in his room.

VIRTUAL PRACTICE: CREATING YOUR DAILY TO-DO LISTS

We asked Colin to share his goals for the upcoming week with us. Here's his week's agenda:

Goals for This Week

Find snake !!!

Ask Kitt to the school dance

Impress Kenny Richards (show him snake)

Pass algebra test

Buy mice (for snake)

Make $$$$ (for Friday dance and to buy mice)

Mail recommendations for football scholarship: Notre Dame, University of Nebraska and University of Iowa

Work on "reptile" collection

Work out

Next we asked Colin to break those weekly goals into daily to-do's. Here's his daily agenda for the week.

Monday To-Do's

FIND SNAKE!!!

Set alarm clock to get up early and go search tool cabinets in garage for snake

Come straight home from school and search laundry area for snake

Investigate "snake traps" (call pet store for safe ideas)

Call Kenny Richards and invite him to come over tomorrow and look at my snake (surely I'll have found it—if not, have him come over and help me search for it)

Find Kitt during lunch and sit with her

Do algebra homework and start studying for Wednesday's test

Work out at gym

Tuesday To-Do's

After school, go to the pet store and buy mice

Come home and feed snake (have Kenny over to watch)

See if Kitt wants to come to the pet store after school

Study for algebra

Call and ask Mr. Walker if he needs me to do any yard work on Saturday

Go to post office and mail football scholarship recommendations

Wednesday To-Do's

Ask Kitt if she'd like to "hang- out" after school

Call and ask Ms. Daniels if she'd like me to wax her car this weekend

Study for algebra

Check out books on collecting reptiles and creating great aquar-iums (terrariums?)

Work out at gym

Thursday To-Do's

Wake up early to eat a good meal and study for the algebra test

At lunch, sit w/Kitt

Get all homework DONE!

Read reptile books (decide what reptile can go in with the snake)

Friday To-Do's

Start on Mr. Walker's yard after school

Ask Kitt to the movies for Saturday

Finish any homework so my weekend is free

Weekend To-Do's

Saturday

Finish Mr. Walker's yard

Wax Ms. Daniels' car

Go to movie with Kitt

Work out at gym

Pet store / check out lizards and terrarium rocks and plants

Sunday

Go to beach

Family dinner—my turn to cook meal

Do my laundry

Hang out w/Kenny and Curt (mall?—check w/Elaine
to see where she and Kitt are hanging out)

Okay, it's time to break your weekly goals into daily to-do's. (Note: you will find a copy of this weekly worksheet in the Appendix. It's labeled Worksheet #5.)

Monday To-Do's

_____

_____

_____

Tuesday To-Do's

_____

_____

_____

_____

_____

_____

_____

Wednesday To-Do's

_____

_____

_____

_____

_____

_____

_____

Thursday To-Do's

_____

_____

_____

_____

_____

_____

_____

_____

Friday To-Do's

_____

_____

_____

_____

_____

_____

_____

_____

Weekend To-Do's

_____

_____

_____

_____

_____

_____

_____

It's Up to You!

Glance at your daily to-do's at the beginning of each morning, refer to it throughout the day, and then review it before you go to bed at night. If you were unable to get something done, you know you need to add it to your to-do's for the next day. And here's a suggestion: Don't toss these out. Keep them in a folder and refer back to them when needed. They'll make for a great log of your activities. Try it; you'll see!

Now that you've had a good chance to look at your goals and to examine the activities necessary to achieve them, can you see any "problems" or major challenges to overcome? If an obstacle stands in the way of meeting your goal, you'll want to remove it so you can get going on making your goal a reality. In this next unit, you'll get a chance to identify any roadblocks between you and your goals, as well as what you can do to remove them. And best of all, you'll learn ways to cheer you on to success in meeting your goals!

Part 5

Just Do It!
Achieving Your
Goals!

You always miss 100 percent of the shots you don't take.
—Source Unknown

Motivation is what gets you started.
Habit is what keeps you going.
—Jim Ryan

Whether you believe you can do a thing or not,
you are right.
—Henry Ford

Today a new sun rises . . . cherish it.
—Anne De Lenclos

There is only one success . . . to be able to spend your
life in your own way.
—Christopher Morley

18

A Message from the Authors

Okay, so you've set out nine great goals you want to accomplish, and you've made a list of the activities necessary to achieve them. You've even broken them into what needs to be done month by month, week by week, and you have a daily agenda firmly in hand. What's left? It's time to check to see if there is anything that stands in the way of you meeting your goals. And that's what this unit is all about: Consider it your "heads up" on making sure there's no "virus" just waiting to "crash" your goals!

If you work on a computer, either at home or at school, maybe you've heard of a computer "virus." A virus is a term given to a "bug" that, like a virus in the human body, moves around within the computer's system, just waiting to infect it. A virus is bad news! If you've been informed that one has made its way into your computer and is now lurking somewhere among your programs and files, you can't ignore it. Should a human contract a virus, with proper medical care, in time most go away. Not so when a computer contracts a computer virus. It has no intentions of going away—although it has grand plans to make all your computer files and programs go away! Sooner or later (and most usually sooner), it's going to crash your computer, and you'll have a crisis on your hands (not to mention losing the time, work and creativity you've put into creating documents—and then the headache of restoring your computer programs).

What "virus" could be lurking among your carefully laid plans for meeting your goals? In a word, *obstacles*. Even with your carefully laid plans, an obstacle, like a virus, can wipe out your best intentions for meeting your goals. Make sure this doesn't happen. If you fail to remove an obstacle, it may stop you from achieving your goals—something that Holly Melvin was wise enough to know about.

One of Holly's goals was to go to college, but she needed financial assistance to pay the tuition. Holly had her heart set on attending a specific university with a great English department (she wants to be a journalist). She carefully filled out the application, as well as all necessary forms to apply for a loan. Planning ahead, she considered the possibility that she might not get accepted to the university and decided that should that be the case, she would go to what she called her Plan B. In her case, Plan B was to attend college at the university that was her second choice. She even had a plan should she not get accepted to that school: She would get her general education units at a junior college, while continuing to apply to universities that offered financial assistance. When Holly got accepted to the university that was her first choice—but didn't end up with the scholarship she needed—we discovered that she even had a backup plan to overcome the obstacle of tuition money. She would secure a loan from her grandfather (which he had agreed to), as well as work part-time while going to school.

Thanks to her thorough planning, Holly is well on her way toward making her dream of going to college come true.

Of course, not all obstacles to meeting your goals are readily apparent. For example, let's say that you and your best friend set a goal to go to "the" concert of the year! You've both worked hard saving the money for the (expensive) tickets, and even spent nearly twelve hours in line to purchase tickets on the day they went on sale. You are both so excited about going. Then, one day before the concert, your friend informs you that a guy she's been dying to go out with asked her to the concert, and while she knows she promised to go with you, she has decided she is going to the concert with him. Friendship issues aside, what are you going to do? She's using her ticket, so it's not like you can see if another friend of yours wants to buy her ticket and the two of you can go. So, do you go to the concert alone, or do you feel "bummed" to the point of deciding not to go at all and, therefore, let the disappointment rob you of your goal of attending the concert? Of course, in such situations only you can decide for yourself, but as you may know, even your own attitude can turn into a "virus"—one that wipes out your goal. Has something like that ever happened to you? Has your attitude stood in the way of your succeeding at a goal? It can happen to anyone. This unit will help you "debug" your own head from any "attitude virus," the goal being to lay claim to a winning attitude so that even a frustrating calamity won't stop you from your goals—and enjoying their rewards!

There comes a time when all the plans are complete and the only thing left is to just set out and do it! After devising a plan for overcoming obstacles in chapter 19, you'll learn how to "debug" your own attitude should it get a virus in chapter 20. Chapter 21 will teach you how to be your own cheerleader. All those plans you've designed in the previous chapters call for concrete action. We're talking about "You can do it!" self-determination.

If you are willing—determined—to make your goals happen, you can and will succeed. Think positive: Believe you can, which as all taste-berry teens know, includes believing in yourself.

Taste Berries to You! Bettie and Jennifer Leigh Youngs

19

Removing Obstacles That Stand in the Way of Meeting Your Goals

The Weekend in the Desert

With finals coming up, what could be better than a little "R&R" and some fun in the sun? When my friend Cory suggested that four of us buddies go on a weekend camping trip to the desert, we all jumped at the idea. My mom wasn't thrilled about it, but being a resourceful guy I found a way to overcome her objections. One of my mom's problems with me going was that we needed a chaperone. We took care of that: We talked our friend Todd's older brother, Kyle, into coming along. This worked out even better for us, since he brought his Jeep and we could go four-wheeling over the sand dunes. Mom was also "concerned" about the time I'd lose from studying for my geography final the following Monday. But I pleaded and promised and studied in advance, and in the end I overcame that objection, too.

If only we could've "overcome" our planning (or lack of planning) for the trip!

Aside from the fact that the desert was way colder at night than we'd imagined it would be (it would've been nice if someone had checked the expected temperatures ahead of time!), our first night wasn't too bad although we all would've slept a little better if we'd been prepared by bringing warmer jackets and thermals. By the time we pulled into camp, it was long after dark, since we had gotten lost along the way and still weren't sure if we were where we were originally headed. (We would have been better off if we had mapped the trip before we got on the road!) I meant to check with AAA (they do have a service for things like this), but unfortunately it remained "another good idea"—and a missed opportunity. Still, it seemed a good enough place to camp—even if it didn't have the extras Cory had told us about. (We probably should have checked out those references after all!) We built a campfire and then got out our sleeping bags and tents and set them up, and by that time, we were so tired, the minute our heads hit the pillow, we were out!

After all, we could hardly wait for sunrise and those sand dunes. The next morning we had breakfast with—well, let's just say we ate the cereal dry. The milk had soured to the point of being curdled, having spoiled on the way there—along with the lunch meat—and you should've smelled the mayonnaise! And if only you could have seen what those twenty candy bars looked like—all melted and running out of their wrappings! It was gross. I knew we should have brought more ice. (Not to mention having agreed on a menu ahead of time and deciding who was bringing what—instead of "everybody bring food.") Still, a little thing like a skimpy breakfast wasn't going to get us down—we had four-wheeling to get to.

We all got in the Jeep and took off over the dunes. "This is what we came for, boys!" Todd hooted as we soared up and down over the dunes. Laughing and hollering we all agreed— having the time of our lives for at least thirty minutes. Then Kyle headed over this one dune, and there on the other side we suddenly found ourselves in a creek bed. We were in the middle of it before anyone knew what had happened. Who would've thought there'd be a creek in the desert? We crashed through some scraggly bushes and reeds, and the tires of the Jeep sank in the squishy muck of the half-dried-out creek bed. Once again, the thought that a map would've been a great purchase crossed my mind. Kyle tried to back us out of the creek bed, and the wheels of the Jeep spun around, splattering mud up over us as we sat in the open bed of the Jeep. Groaning and wiping the mud off ourselves, we jumped from the Jeep and tried to push it from the creek bed. Kyle tried to pull first forward, then backward, spraying plumes of mud over all of us. "Watch out!" we howled, swiping the mud from our eyes and spitting it from our mouths. Meanwhile, we were standing almost up to our ankles in the smelly muck. It didn't take an engineer to see we were only digging ourselves in deeper.

"We'll have to go back to camp and get Josh's car to go get a tow," Kyle said, as he climbed from the Jeep. Suddenly, Dan, who was shaking the mud from his body, looked at Todd and I doing the same and started laughing. At that point, even as we grunted and moaned at being in such a mess, we all started laughing at how we looked. We laughed and laughed as we walked out of the mud and along the bushes at the side of the creek. Suddenly, Todd, who was leading our trek, stopped laughing and froze. Dan piled into the back of him. "Hey, what'd you stop for?" Dan scowled. Too late, he saw the skunk. It sprayed in our direction, tagging Todd and Dan. I'm here to tell you that climbing the desert dunes back to camp was anything but relaxing, besides being just plain no fun. And I probably don't have to tell you that no, we hadn't purchased the "what to do should you get sprayed by a skunk" manual!

By the time we made it back to camp, we were all already exhausted. Then, by the time Josh and Kyle returned with the tow truck and got the Jeep out of the mud and back to the campsite, it was time to crawl into our sleeping bags for the night. But even after trying to clean up with what water we had, crawling into our sleeping bags just wasn't happening—especially not for Todd and Dan. Besides it felt like it was nearly freezing! Add to that the fact that the canned food and potato chips just weren't hitting the spot, we all voted to drive home where we could take a good hot shower, eat something tasty and sleep in our own beds.

If there's a moral to my story (which I'm not saying there necessarily is), I would have to say that it's either: Even the best-laid plans have to leave room for being flexible (like going home early), or When it comes to the best-laid plans, make sure you make them! I did make some points with Mom, though. When she asked why I was home early, I replied, "Mom, remember me telling you about my final in geography on Monday? Well, I wanted to make sure I had enough time to study without any distractions."

Mitch Reneir, 17

What Stands in the Way of You Meeting Your Goals?

Mitch certainly ran into a few unforeseen obstacles on his camping trip, some of which could have been anticipated—and overcome—beforehand! Whether you're working on your goals for the month, the week or the day, before you set off on your goal, brainstorm what you see as obstacles that could get in the way of reaching your goals. The more obstacles you can identify up front, the better chance you will have to accomplish your goals. Here are three important questions to ask:

1. Is there anything that stands in the way of my achieving this goal?
2. If so, what can I do to remove the obstacles?
3. Do I need help and, if so, who can I ask (and what will I ask of this person)?

VIRTUAL PRACTICE: THREE EASY STEPS TO REMOVING OBSTACLES

Step #1: What obstacles stand in the way of achieving my goals? Identify what stands between you and your goal. For this, you'll want to get out your paper and pencil and list any foreseeable obstacles. Initially, Mitch identified this one:

1) My mother said I couldn't go (because an "unchaperoned" outing for four seventeen-year-olds could be dangerous and she felt I needed the weekend as a time to study for the upcoming final)!

As you read Mitch's story, you can see he faced some real obstacles, but this one appeared to be a "deal-breaker" in and of itself! Mitch was determined to go and set about removing this obstacle and did. After reading his story, we also know there were others. In hindsight, he developed these:

1) We didn't know exactly where the campsite was located.
2) The desert was very cold at night.
3) The food was awful—we should have taken better "camping" food, or called around and found where the fast-food places were located.

Step #2: What can I do to remove the obstacles? After identifying barriers that stand between you and your goal, decide what you can do to overcome each one. We already know how Mitch tackled the one obstacle he identified as his mother being worried about an "unchaperoned outing for four seventeen-year-olds."

To overcome his mother's objections, he reassured her by inviting Todd's older brother, Kyle, to chaperone.

Now, let's look at a couple of those obstacles that Mitch failed to take into account (but identified in hindsight) and see how he might've overcome them:

Obstacle: We didn't know exactly where the campsite was located.

To overcome the obstacle:

- ♥ *I could buy a map—or make sure that Cory bought one.*
- ♥ *I could go online and print out a map.*

Obstacle: The desert was very cold at night.
To overcome the obstacle:

- ♥ *I could listen to weather reports.*
- ♥ *I could go online and look up weather reports.*
- ♥ *After learning about the weather, I could bring warmer clothes, thermals, coats, etc.*

Obstacle: The food was awful.
To overcome the obstacle:

- ♥ *We could have done a food plan—basically, planning a daily menu in order to anticipate the amount of food needed (or found out in advance what restaurants and fast-food facilities were within driving distance of the campsite).*

Step #3: Do I need help in removing the obstacles and, if so, who can I ask to help me remove obstacles (and what will I ask of that person)? Here you identify those who can help you remove the obstacles to meeting your particular goals. As you know from reading Mitch's account of his weekend, he enlisted the help of Todd's older brother, Kyle.

Now let's consider how he might've gotten help with those obstacles he failed to consider:

Obstacle: We didn't know exactly where the campsite was located.

To overcome the obstacle:

♥ <u>We could talk to Cory's parents about how to reach the campsite (since he said it was where his family had gone).</u>

♥ <u>I could call the local park and recreation department rangers and ask for directions to camps—and for good, safe four-wheeling trails.</u>

Obstacle: The desert was very cold at night.

To overcome the obstacle:

♥ <u>I could call the local park and recreation department rangers and ask about camping in the desert and what the weather was like.</u>

♥ <u>I could borrow my brother's down sleeping bag.</u>

Obstacle: We ran out of food.

To overcome the obstacle:

♥ <u>I could ask my mom what kind of meals are easy to make when you're out in camping conditions—and then if she'd help me write down a menu.</u>

Okay, it's time for you to apply this process. In the space below, write down one of your more "intense" goals for the month at hand.

Goal: _____

_____

STEP #1: What obstacle stands in the way of my achieving my goal?

♥ Obstacle: _____

_____

_____

STEP #2: What can I do to remove this obstacle?

I could: _____

_____

_____

STEP #3: Do I need help removing this obstacle and, if so, who can I ask and specifically, what will I ask of that person?

I will ask _____ to help me by _____

_____

(Note: An extra copy of this worksheet is provided for your use in the Appendix. It is labeled Worksheet #6.)

It's Up to You!

A well-laid course is your best defense against any obstacle that life may throw your way. Just as when it comes to being prepared for a big test or not having studied for it, the same holds true with reaching your goals: The better prepared you are—having studied all angles—the better your chance of success.

Up until now, you've received an array of practical "traveling tools" for reaching your goals. Now, fully prepared, it's time for you to go for it—take charge and tackle your goals. You can do it! We believe in you! The following chapter will give you the encouragement to believe in yourself (just in case you don't already do that on a regular basis).

You Can Do It! (So Do It!)

An Acrophobic's Plunge!

"Go ahead, jump!" a buddy of mine taunted, and then dared, "Bet you won't!" I looked into the water from where I was standing and knew he was probably right. Standing practically on the top of the world, or at least it seemed that way to me, and thinking of plunging into the depths of an endless ocean below, I was scared to death! I'm an acrophobic (I have a fear of heights), so you can imagine the chill that went down my spine as I considered the possibilities of taking up the dare. I moved closer to the edge of the three-thousand-foot-high platform to take a better look at the distance "down" and began thinking (which is probably the worst thing I could have done):

"You can do it!" one voice coaxed.

"No, you fool! You'll kill yourself!" warned another.

"Oh, go on! Do it!" the first one prodded.

"But you've never done this before!" pleaded the more sane voice.

"That's because you always play it safe," mocked the first.

"You can't," said the second voice.

"C'mon! Don't wimp out—jump!" taunted the first. I hate losing to that voice—so I jumped!

The good news is, I'm alive to tell the story!

Okay, let me tell you that I didn't jump three thousand feet. It was more like three hundred feet. Well, in truth, it was actually thirty feet—but it most definitely felt like three thousand to me. And since I'm setting the record straight, the jump wasn't from the "top of the world," but rather, from a yacht on which I was a guest. But just so you can empathize, you should know that a crowd of nearly fifty pretty cool "peers" from various teen organizations stood watching—many of whom were friends and classmates from my own school! All were looking to see if I'd take the bait of jumping off the yacht and into the water. What could I do?

Even though I didn't want to jump, how does someone say "no" when everyone in the whole world is watching? I mean, if I hadn't proven myself as in, "I can do this, no sweat!" I'd never live it down. I'm sure you know the feeling. As I stood there looking down into the water, I cannot describe the fear I felt knowing I just had to jump. It seemed more like suicide than heroics to me. I mean, I can swim, so it's not like jumping meant automatic death by drowning, but I really am terrified of heights. The fear of free-falling so far down snapped me to my senses, and I backed away. No way was I going to jump! But then I remembered that voice saying, "You always play it safe . . . ," and something in me just let loose. In a split-second, I whirled around, took a ten-foot running start and vaulted into the air!

Here's the thing: The jump was a moment I will never, ever forget. In that instant so many things went racing through my head—like death, for instance—but taking the plunge was absolutely, positively and completely exhilarating, too. Sailing through midair on my way into a bottomless ocean, it occurred to me that my entire life had been lived with reservation. Everything was structured; the clock ruled my life. I lived a boring schedule of predictable activity. Why did I always play it safe? Living life that way was as useless as using a flashlight in broad daylight. No more. Sailing through the air on my jump that day, I vowed that from here on out, I was going to "Go for it!" I was put on this planet to live, not just breathe. As the ocean grew closer to my face, I realized the difference.

I hit the water.

It was baptizing. I emerged from the water a different person, and not just because I had jumped off the boat, but also because in the seconds it took for me to go from the top of the yacht to the water, I'd become a courageous person. And in that moment, I understood I must live bravely from here on out. Now, when I hear a voice inside my head trying to hold me back or limit me—by causing me to doubt myself, or by reminding me of times when I failed at something—I remind myself of that voice that said, "C'mon! Don't wimp out—jump!" I don't mean to say that I take unnecessary risks, but I have decided to go for it. And that has made all the difference. And I'm not as scared of heights as I once used to be. I do have more courage and bravery than I've ever had in my life. All because of that one jump! It's created a real goal: My goal is to be courageous and not so afraid to take risks. Since I know that I can overcome my acrophobia enough to jump from thirty feet, I know I can face just about any fear that comes my way. Just knowing that helps me believe in myself, and now that I believe in myself, I'm determined to face my fears and meet the challenges when it comes to reaching all the goals in my life.

Mike Siciliano, 18

Be Determined: Go for It!

Mike was determined to "take the plunge"—even in the face of his greatest fear. Now that's determination! Sometimes the "leap" you have to take is one of faith—faith in yourself and your ability to succeed in meeting your goals no matter what challenges you face.

The following are some ways to increase your "You can do it, so do it!" confidence.

- ♥ **Believe in yourself.** Although, of course, we hope to have others cheer us on toward our goals, the most valuable cheerleader of all is the one who is with you literally all of the time—yourself. Not only are there those times when you're all alone with your goals, unfortunately there are also those days when others may not believe in you. Sixteen-year-old Arianna Rueben had just such an experience. "I am a high-school junior, and I wanted to be president of the student body more than anyone else ever realized," Arianna told us in a recent workshop. "I just knew I would make the best president the school could ever have. Well, a junior had never before been president of the student body at my school. What's more, most of the former presidents had been guys. Even though my friends pitched in and helped me with my campaign, they all told me I was fighting a losing battle. But I refused to believe that I couldn't meet my goal, and today—you guessed it— I'm president of my high school's student body!"

  Arianna is a shining example of how the ability to believe in yourself can help you accomplish your goals. Arianna makes it clear that you should never underestimate your own power to achieve your goals—or the importance in believing that you can.
- ♥ **Be optimistic and hopeful.** Our hopes move us forward in life as they give us a vision, a reason to try, a goal to move toward. "What I hoped for most was a little privacy. My parents work really hard, but there are five of us kids and there are some things there just isn't money to buy. A bigger

house is definitely one of them," Chaz Collins wrote. "I got so tired of sharing my room with both of my brothers. All I wanted was a room of my own, my own private space. I wouldn't let myself even consider the possibility that it wouldn't happen. I could clearly picture it with its walls plastered with the posters I wanted to hang. But I didn't have any great insights into how to make it happen, even though I always believed that it eventually would. Then, one summer day, I went to work with my dad. He's in construction and he was remodeling someone's home. As I helped him, I looked at the space and what it took to put up walls, and an amazing thought occurred to me—I could do this with my bedroom! I just knew I could. I worked with my dad over the summer and made enough extra money to buy the drywall and lumber to put up dividers in my room—so I have my very own space. My dad helped, and while we were at it, we gave my brothers dividers, too. Still my space is the coolest. It's not a room of my own—not yet—but it's close and it's definitely a 'space' of my own."

Chaz remained forever optimistic and hopeful no matter how unlikely his dream of having his own "space" seemed. This gave him the attitude needed to make his hopes and dreams realities, as it put him in a "space" of believing in himself and going for it!

♥ **Hang around positive people.** Keep company with those who inspire and uplift you. It helps you to do your best and be your best. As fifteen-year-old Kendra Hansen explained, "My best friend Elisa is the most optimistic person on the planet. It's one of the reasons I so enjoy being with her. Whenever I'm doubting myself or having a trying time, she's right there, absolutely believing that everything is going to turn out 'as destined.' She reminds me that I can get through it by telling me, 'See yourself getting through this, because you will.' She says that about any goal that either of us sets—from her going out with Todd Granger, to me getting the job I wanted at the record store. And you know what? We actually do reach our goals. I honestly feel being around Elisa and her positive attitude is a huge part of believing in myself enough to get through tough times, as well as setting and achieving some amazing goals."

♥ **Do what it takes to make your dreams come true.** You're sure to boost your belief in yourself if you're diligent in doing all that you can to achieve success. Mariah Mitchell set passing chemistry with an A as her goal for the semester. "The class turned out to be so much harder than I expected, but an A was my goal and I was determined to get it," Mariah said. "It all came down to whether I could pull in an A on my final, and I was a little worried. I decided to increase my chances of success by totally doing my part: I prepared for the test (studied, studied, studied). When my friend Leah called the night before the final, I didn't let her talk about a rumor about who my ex-boyfriend asked out because I knew that if I did, I would get worked up and I wouldn't be able to fall asleep, then I wouldn't be at my best the next day. I got a good night's sleep that night, and in the morning, I ate a good breakfast. Knowing I'd given it my all gave me the self-confidence I needed to get that A. P.S. I did get an A!"

♥ **Look out for your self-esteem.** Enhancing your self-esteem means doing those things that make you feel good about yourself. We enhance our self-esteem when we have integrity—when we say and behave in ways that lead to setting and achieving worthwhile goals. "In the seventh grade, I started hanging around with a few guys who used BB guns to shoot birds off the telephone wires and who wrote dirty words with felt markers on the windows of parked cars. Of course, I did it, too," Brent Cross admitted. "I can tell you, I didn't feel very good about myself. When

I actually hit one of the birds, then I felt downright guilty. What's more, my grades at school dropped. I just didn't seem to have it in me to do my best; worse yet, I didn't even want to try. In the summer between seventh and eighth grade, I went to stay with my grandparents and became friends with the kids who lived on their street. They did other things for fun, like skateboarding and swimming. It felt good to be doing things I didn't have to feel guilty about. So when I came home after the summer, I quit hanging around with the guys I'd been hanging around with and made new friends. And that year all my grades came up. I know it was because I felt good about myself as a person."

♥ **Don't let a failure throw you off-course.** A failure is not the end of the world. Know that you'll survive and can even thrive through those times you don't succeed. If things don't work out the way you had hoped, don't be down on yourself for moping around a few days; just don't let yourself stay in that space too long. "I wanted to be a cheerleader my entire life," Gracie Franklin claimed. "I watched cheerleaders on television, took gymnastics to learn cheerleader routines and moves, made up my own cheers and dreamed of the day I could be a cheerleader. When I finally got old enough to go out for cheerleading, I practiced all summer so I'd be ahead of the game when it came to tryouts. But after all that, I didn't make cheerleader. I was devastated. I know that I did everything I could—nobody could possibly have done more. I didn't even have an appetite for two whole days. Finally, I realized there was always next year. I just had to pick myself up and do some cheerleading for myself. Next year, I'm going out for cheerleading again. I have every faith next year I'll make the squad." It can be expected that you'll feel down and low when at first you don't succeed. So give yourself a little time to "get over it" and then get up and go once again. If you want a real "pick-me-up," ask anyone you know who is successful how many times they experienced "failures" along the way. As you'll no doubt learn, they'll list a good number of "false starts" and failed attempts. That's just the way it is.

There are lots of ways to increase your "you can do it, so do it!" confidence in reaching your goals. You can never have too much inspiration and motivation—especially trying to overcome any challenges that stand in the way of your goals.

Mike Siciliano's story helps you see how facing your fears can grant you the experience, confidence and strength of character you need to keep striving for your goals. Facing those fears and remaining determined can sometimes take all the inspiration and motivation you can muster, so you'll want to develop truly great skills for motivating and inspiring yourself. The following questions will help you become clear on just how to do this.

VIRTUAL PRACTICE: HOW TO BE AN INSPIRATION TO YOURSELF

List three good reasons why you can believe in yourself! (These can be three successes you've achieved, three goals you've accomplished or three of your great qualities.)

_____

_____

_____

Do you consider yourself an optimistic person? Explain.

_____

Who are the three most optimistic people you know? What are some of their favorite words and ways to inspire and encourage you?

How do you "do what it takes" when you doubt yourself? Give an example of a time when you cheered yourself on after suffering a "defeat."

What do you do to look out for your self-esteem? Give an example.

What are your favorite and most effective "cheers"? What do you tell yourself to keep you moving toward your goals in spite of setbacks or when you need to build your own confidence?

_____

_____

_____

_____

It's Up to You!

Sometimes achieving a goal takes that "no matter what" kind of drive. In the following, final chapter, you'll see how Jennifer kept herself "horsepower-charged" to reach her goals "no matter what." As her story unfolds, you'll also learn how important it is that you, like Jennifer, "see" yourself as successful in order to "be" successful in meeting your goals.

Get a Life: Make It Happen!

The Horse for Horsepower Exchange . . .

I fell in love with horses at the age of six. It was then that I was first hoisted into the leather saddle of a Shetland paint pony by the name of Nippers. It was at the Iowa State Fair—a dream haven for horse lovers because of all the equestrian events held there each year. In spite of a sore rear from riding that day and not knowing how to ride properly, somewhere in the first few minutes of being on that horse, I made it my goal to one day own a horse of my own.

My mother was against the whole idea: "They're huge, dangerous animals and extremely expensive," she said when I presented her with the idea of owning a horse. Pleading didn't work so I tried begging, but it didn't matter. Mom didn't want a horse in my (or her) already overtaxed schedule. "We've got enough things to do, to feed and to take care of," she said, reminding me of the time needed for homework, piano lessons and Girl Scouts, as well as two kittens, a hamster, dog, lizard, two parakeets and a tank of goldfish. "But I take good care of all of them," I reasoned. Wanting to wrap up our "discussion" on having a horse join our family's cast of characters, Mom countered with, "If you want a horse, put it on your goal list and make it happen."

So then I knew that my owning a horse was a possibility: A master "goal achiever" herself, it was my mother who had taught me how to set, and go after, goals!

Throughout my childhood, at the start of each semester, my mother would take a piece of tag board and, sitting together at the kitchen table, she'd say to me, "Jennifer, what are the six most important things you'd like to have happen this school year?" Of course, she followed this question with, "For example, your goal for good friends, for liking your teachers, for getting good grades, for playing sports and keeping your room clean—and then for one other extra-special something (such as getting a new bike this year)." If you think those became my goals each year, you'd be right!

To this explanation of the "importance of setting goals for the year," my mother also offered a visual as a way for me to "see" my progress in their achievement. After a discussion of why each goal was important, I got to draw a large circle on the piece of tag board (labeled, "MY GOALS") and write my goal beneath it—such as, "I want to have good friends." Then sometime during the school year, my mother would take a photo of me "doing" or "having met" my goal, and paste it within the circle. Such was the case with cool photos of me being with friends, me holding up a good report card, me riding a new bike, me getting braces (and two years later, getting them off!), me getting a driver's license, me going on my first date and the like.

For the most part, I really enjoyed this activity, especially if she tied rewards to me reaching my goal—as was true each year as I got older. For example, my mother would reward all grades with a certain dollar amount, including deducting for D's and F's. As I recall, I made a lot of money on her system (although I once had to pay her handsomely for a couple of D's!). And every year my allowance increased, along with my hourly wage when I worked in my mother's office. So there were some real good perks to her system, and as long as it worked in my favor, I never complained.

But of all the goals, it was the last category (the "extra-special something") that I found most exciting (both as a young kid and when in junior high and high school). It was also the category that held out the most promise for my goal of owning a horse. While getting a new bike took up that slot one year, I was really careful not to damage that bike, and I made sure it didn't need too many new chains or tires. Once I'd set the goal for owning a horse, I didn't want to use up another entire year for "something extra-special" on things like repairing a bike. I wanted a horse—and my mother wasn't keen on my having one, so I was on my own in getting one in my life. But my mother never intruded on—or rejected—what it was that I wanted as my "something extra-special." And so, in fourth grade I wrote, "Getting to go riding every Saturday" in the "extra-special something" slot. While my mother protested, she also allowed it.

I was on my way!

Over the next couple of years, I rode horses on the weekend at a little ranch called Peppertree Farms. I loved it and spent a lot of time there, so much so that my mother called it my "home away from home." I got really good at riding, learning both the English and Western style of riding, as well as bareback. But I learned other things as well: Some fifty horse owners boarded their horses at Peppertree Farms, which made it prudent for a local veterinarian to come every Saturday morning to check in on sick or injured horses and sometimes to provide wellness checks. I was a quick study: Learning about caring for a horse was of great interest to me. After all, I was on a mission to own one!

And so it was that I learned how to groom and care for and properly feed a horse. I also learned what to do if a horse got injured on the trail or bitten by a snake. It's a lot of work caring for a horse, and not all of it is glamorous. Picking the crud out of a horse's hoofs (necessary so they don't get hoof rot or other foot diseases), brushing their teeth and worming them are necessary chores, whether you like doing them or not. I learned how expensive it is to board a horse, not to mention the cost of saddles, riding blankets, treats and being sure they get good food and hay and adequate vitamins and minerals. But I got good at asking for "supplies" in exchange for favors, good behavior, and as gifts for special occasions. It got to the point where a hoof pick in my stocking at Christmas really made my day.

While at Peppertree Farms one particularly beautiful spring morning when I was in sixth grade, I spotted a "For Lease" sign on the stall of a horse I'd grown to like. Noticing that the monthly lease on the horse amounted to less than the daily amount I was paying for riding each weekend, I quickly told my mother of the "savings of leasing on a monthly basis, rather than renting on a daily basis." It made sense to her, too. So I leased the horse and was moving up in the world in terms of meeting my goal for owning a horse of my own. And when the very horse I was leasing (and had fallen in love with) was being offered for sale by the owner, I added up what I would save by owning the horse rather than leasing it and quickly informed my mother. But she was a hard sell on this and told me, "If you can pay for it, you can own it."

I saw myself as an owner of my own horse. I was so determined to not let anything get in my way of accomplishing that goal. I also knew I needed to move fast—the owner wanted to sell the horse. One small problem: I didn't have enough money. So I made a plan: I'd ask my mother to contribute the money she paid for the rental on a monthly basis times twelve months. My birthday was coming up, and Dad and both my grandparents always gave me money—so I'd let them know how terribly expensive a horse was—and reassure them I couldn't exist without a horse in my life. As for the tooth fairy leaving a dollar per tooth—well, that wouldn't do. Ten dollars was surely more fair—so when the very next tooth fell out, I wrote a letter and Scotch-taped the tooth to the "bill" for having gone through the loss of the tooth in the first place. You might say that I got very creative in finding ways to get the things I needed for my expensive but necessary "horse habit" as my mother called it. I bartered everything from doing favors to good behavior for supplies, as well as negotiated some pretty successful hauls of grain and other supplies with Santa Claus, the Easter Bunny, Cupid, generous grandparents and relatives alike.

I saw myself as moving toward my goal—and I was: When I was twelve, my mother took a picture of me sitting atop my beautiful horse, Brockton—one I owned—and we pasted it to the "something extra-special" that year. To date, it's been one of the sweetest victories—goals—I've accomplished.

Brockton was the best horse in the world *because* he was mine, all mine. Trail after trail we rode, Brockton a happy camper and me smiling the entire way, enjoying the "fruits of my labor." My horse and I were a team and together we entered some shows and won our share of ribbons! For those of you who love to ride, I don't have to tell you the thrill of soaring amidst nature with the wind and sun in your face on a two-ton machine of toned muscle and pure grace. It's a magical feeling. Go for a horse ride. It'll clear your mind and renew your soul!

At seventeen, my priorities changed, and I exchanged my desire for a horse for a desire for horsepower (a car). As usual, when I expressed an interest in (okay, when I begged) for a car, my mother proclaimed her usual, "If you can pay for it, you can own it."

And so it was that I sold my beloved horse. Even though this was my decision, I cried and cried over losing him, taking great care to see that he went to a loving new owner—which he did. I then used the money I earned from the sale as a down payment on a magnificent new Mitsubishi. Then, with yet a new goal in place—to afford the monthly loan payments—I started a part-time job. But once again bliss was mine: I loved having wheels of my own, and since I picked out the car, it was a goal of my heart's choosing. I drove the car for a million years, and on the day I sold it, though it was by now a relic with a zillion miles on it, I cried and cried as they drove away with my precious vehicle.

While I have a different car, I don't have a horse, but each year, I'm missing it more and more. So much so that I'm thinking of adding getting a horse to my goals this year—and yes, I'll put it in that circle called, "Something extra-special"—and on a tag-board chart that I make on my own and hang on the wall in my study.

So I'm glad that my mother taught me to set goals in the way that she did. To her, goals were about bringing about achievement in the most basic and important areas of life: good friends, good relationships, achievement at work or school, and "something extra-special."

So setting goals and achieving them is something I'm fond of doing. Best of all, from my personal experience of achieving goals I've set (yes, there have been a few of those I haven't reached as well), I have a lot of confidence that I can have those things I want in life. I'm convinced that when I decide on something I want and focus energy on how to attain it, I can and will make it happen. As a result, I see myself as a capable person—which is a direct outcome of having achieved my goals.

I've learned there's no such thing as a dream too big to bring about. Everything is possible. When I was little and would go to my mother with a problem that needed (my) resolution, we'd talk about it and she'd say, "Before you go to bed, put it in your mind's eye, and tell yourself you're looking to find the best possible solution—that will put the wheels of your mind in motion, so to speak, and in the morning, you'll have an answer." Her method always seemed to work! I've learned that the same process is important for seeing yourself as capable in bringing about your goals.

I've heard that "seeing is believing," but when it comes to my goals I've learned that believing is "seeing." Over the years, I also made a believer out of my mother, but more importantly, I made a believer out of me.

Jennifer Leigh Youngs

See It, Believe It, Achieve It

As we saw in Jennifer's story, setting your goals and then focusing on doing those things required to make them happen changes those goals into accomplishments. By now you've identified and prioritized your goals, and then gone on to chart them out in daily, weekly and monthly to-do's. Each of these steps is important; each moves you closer to your goals and makes it easier for you to see what you need to do to achieve them. Remember Jennifer's tag board with the shapes for each of her goals? This gave Jennifer a definite destination that she could actually see as she set out to "make each of her goals happen." This "map" was her cheerleader encouraging her to meet her dreams.

One of Jennifer's goals was to get her braces removed by prom time, a goal her dentist told her was possible if she was diligent in caring for her teeth each day, which included not only daily hygiene, but tightening the bands on her braces each day (which could be very uncomfortable). Even on days when Jennifer was tempted to skip tightening her braces, one glance at her "dream map" (where she had taped a picture of a beautiful smile with gleaming, straight teeth), would motivate her to tighten her braces. When you have your goal in front of you, you can more clearly see when you're on or off course. So when you're off course, you're able to correct it and tell yourself, "Come on, you can do it, so do it!" And when you're on course, you're able to feel the thrill of satisfaction that you deserve and tell yourself, "Right on! You're awesome!" What's most important is to maintain your attitude for success—to believe in your ability to achieve your goal. One key to keeping up your winning attitude is to make certain you reward yourself for a job well done. Three reasons why acknowledging your accomplishment is important is because it helps you see that:

♥ **You are a capable, competent person.** You identified what you wanted, you went out to get it and you got it. When you accomplish something you have set out to achieve, you see yourself as capable, and you believe in your ability to be goal-oriented.

♥ **You have high self-esteem.** Self-esteem is the reputation you have with you, regardless of what others think of you. You know firsthand what you deserve. You have decided to accomplish something, worked hard to achieve it and met your goal. You know you are worthy, and your self-esteem shoots toward the stars.

♥ **You are a winner.** You've been successful. You deserve a trophy. Whether it's having your name published in the school paper for an award you received, making the honor roll, or earning a letter for your letter jacket, all indicate you are an achiever. Don't forget to reward yourself. Whether you give yourself a new CD, buy new Rollerblades or splurge on concert tickets, when you play the CD, go skating or look back on having been to the concert, you will connect it to the goal you achieved. It serves as a reminder that you're cool!

VIRTUAL PRACTICE: CREATING YOUR DREAM MAP

This exercise is sure to get both sides of your brain in on the action of making your dreams come true. It helps assure that you, like Jennifer, are able to "see, believe and achieve" your goals. How does it do this? It places your dream destinations—your goals—in sight, and then allows you to mark your victories when you've achieved them. This will cheer you on and give you a sense of direction. What's more, with your goals marked on the map right in front of you, you'll know when you're on course and you can reward yourself for your success. Here are instructions for making your own "dream map":

♥ Get a piece of tag board (or poster board). Draw nine shapes, one for each of your nine goals (these can be circles, triangles, squares or stars). You probably won't want them all to be the same shape. And you'll want to make sure each shape is big enough to hold any token of success you'll want to place in it later. (For example, if your goal is to get good grades, make sure the shape where it's written has enough room to hold a copy of your "winning" report card.)

♥ Take your #1 goal in each of the nine goal areas and write a goal below each of the shapes, until you've written a goal below each of the nine. If at all possible, put a picture inside the shape that reminds you of your goal (such as Jennifer did with the smile).

♥ Hang your tag board up in your room or bathroom, anywhere you can see it each day!

♥ When you reach your goals, mark your success in the corresponding shape (whether you do this by taping in a picture of you and your date at the prom, if your goal had been to go to the prom; or by pasting in your first paycheck stub, if your goal had been to get your first part-time job). Don't limit yourself on what you put into the shapes; your trophies and tokens are for you, so you can use whatever you want—as long as it reminds you that you've been successful.

We've included quotes and slogans you can use on your map. Write them in the empty area around your goal spaces. Now is the time to allow your creativity free rein; bring out the magic markers, glitter and paint. You can also flip through magazines to find pictures that inspire you or remind you of your goals and paste those pictures around them.

Remember, there are no limitations in deciding what you'd like to put on your map to remind you of your goals and your success in achieving them. It's your very own inspiration and reminders, your personal "dream map" for reaching your goals. Pull out all stops and have fun charting your journey!

Think big!

The sky's the limit!

Reach for the stars!

Make it happen!

I made it happen!

You can do it!

"Just do it!"

I did it!

I'm cool!

Good work!

Wonderful!

Awesome!

Alllllllright!

Good job!

Way to go!

Excellent!

You did it!

I knew I could do it!

Cool!

What a taste-berry!

Epilogue:
A Closing Word from the Authors

We hope this book has been helpful in giving you the "tools" for setting goals and achieving what you'd like to accomplish. As you can see, thinking about goals you find worth pursuing, and then creating a plan for making them happen, is an important yet simple process. As with many things, the most difficult part is the follow-through. So now it's up to you to follow through on your plans, and to muster up the determination and discipline of staying true to your plan of action. In a word, it's up to you to accomplish your goals.

Always remember, if you stray off course from time to time (which is an easy and perfectly human thing to do), encourage yourself to get back on track. Think of each day as a new beginning. So if you're off course, don't waste your time regretting, finding fault or looking for an excuse. As the saying goes, "Nothing is as far away as a minute ago." Get in gear: Get back to your plan to accomplish what you find important and worthwhile.

We'd also like to remind you that although there have been many steps laid out for your journey in setting and achieving your goals, you should take those steps one at a time. Don't let yourself get overwhelmed. That's the value of setting goals in the first place: You have a plan that guides your activities—you know what you should be doing and when you're supposed to do it. This is a good thing, because it's all too easy to get caught up in an "activity trap"—of being busy, but not necessarily productive. Again, this is why it's important to set goals and to develop a plan for achieving them. We do. We know the value of setting goals, and we know that we'd never accomplish the things we want to do without goals and a plan for reaching them. For example, one of our goals in our Career/Work categories is to continue writing books for our growing *Taste Berries for Teens* series. We follow the same process we've recommended in this book.

We decided to show you a sample of our goal plan in this area, so that you can see that, from the time we first speak to our publisher about doing a new book to the time the book is in your hands, many steps have been put in place to reach our goal. In fact, from just that one goal (to write a new book for our teen series), an entire year's worth of activities—all broken into monthly, weekly and daily goals—have taken place. (You'll note that we do our goals September 1 to September 1.) Here's a brief look:

Overall Career/Work Goals
for September 1, 2001 to September 1, 2002

♥ Support our new books in the *Taste Berries for Teens* series: *A Taste-Berry Teen's Guide to Managing the Stress and Pressures of Life, Taste Berries for Teens #3: Inspirational Stories and Encouragement on Life, Love, Friends and the Face in the Mirror* and *A Taste-Berry Teen's Guide to Setting & Achieving Goals.*

♥ Do ten to fifteen workshops for teens nationwide.

♥ Work with teens within schools nationwide.

♥ Plan and write a new book for the *Taste Berries for Teens* series.

Yearly Goals: Month-at-a-Glance

September 2001:

♥ Our book, *A Taste-Berry Teen's Guide to Managing the Stress and Pressures of Life,* arrives in bookstores! YEAH! We'll reward ourselves with a four-day weekend in Sedona! Yeeeeessssss!

♥ Set up a conference call with our publisher to determine interest in our ideas for a new book for next year—discuss theme, content and title. (We're suggesting, *A Taste-Berry Teen's Guide to Setting & Achieving Goals.*)

October 2001:

♥ It's a go! Our publisher said "Yes!" to our idea on "Goals" as a new book in our series for teens! Follow up to get the contract.

♥ Do the scheduled six-city book tour for *A Taste-Berry Teen's Guide to Managing the Stress and Pressures of Life.*

♥ Think over and plan out the scope of a new "Goals" book for teens; consider best title for book and possible units/chapters.

November 2001:

♥ Refine chapter titles and a draft of chapter outlines for the "Goals" book.

♥ Look over list of former teen contributors and possible new contributors (get in touch with them).

♥ Continue clarifying theme and content for each unit.

♥ Develop one-page overview of book for teens wanting to write for our new book.

♥ E-mail it to select teen contributors.

December 2001:

- ♥ Notify ten to twenty schools to work with teens within English and creative-writing classes.
- ♥ Begin draft of "A Message from the Authors" sections for the "Goals" book.
- ♥ Begin draft of unit 1, first chapter.

January 2002:

- ♥ Develop draft for units 1 to 3 of "Goals" book.
- ♥ Discuss getting a contract from our publisher for adding a new title to our teen series, *A Taste-Berry Teen's Guide to Living Drug-Free.*
- ♥ Correspond with teen contributors.
- ♥ "Goals" book: Write, write, write!

February 2002:

- ♥ Write units 4 to 5 of "Goals" book.
- ♥ Correspond with teen contributors.
- ♥ "Goals" book: Write, write, write!
- ♥ Publisher said "Yes!" to the "Drug-Free" book. Do an initial chapter outline for the book.

March 2002:

- ♥ Second edit for units 1 to 5 (all chapters).
- ♥ Correspond with teen contributors.
- ♥ Meet with our teen editorial review board.
- ♥ Edit, edit, edit!

April 2002:

- ♥ Our new title, *Taste Berries for Teens #3,* is due in book stores! Yes! Reward ourselves with a three-day hiking trip in the mountains!
- ♥ Final edit for units 1 to 5 (all chapters) of "Goals" book.
- ♥ Mail completed "Goals" manuscript off to our publisher.
- ♥ Begin back cover copy.
- ♥ Take photograph for back cover book jacket.
- ♥ Discuss with publisher and editorial staff if a publicity tour is planned for this book.
- ♥ Plan and begin first draft of chapter for the "Drug-Free" book.

May 2002:

- ♥ Attend BEA (Book Expo of America) in New York to sign books for booksellers and other conference attendees.
- ♥ Correspond with teens, letting them know of selection as a "published" author.
- ♥ Continue writing "Drug-Free" book.

June 2002:

- ♥ Speak at the Teen Time National Conference.
- ♥ Meet with our teen editorial review board.
- ♥ Continue writing "Drug-Free" book.

July 2002:

- ♥ Review list of former teen contributors and possible new contributors.
- ♥ Second draft completed for all chapters of "Drug-Free" book.

August 2002:

♥ Set up a conference call with our publisher to determine their interest in a book for our *Taste Berries for Teens* series. Discuss theme, content, suggested table of contents and possible book title.

♥ Turn in completed manuscript for *A Taste-Berry Teen's Guide to Living Drug-Free*.

September 2002:

♥ A *Taste-Berry Teen's Guide to Setting & Achieving Goals* arrives in bookstores! Yeeesssss! Reward ourselves with a four-day trip to San Miguel de Allende, Mexico!

♥ Our publisher said "yes" to our new book idea!

♥ Develop one-page overview of this new book for teens wanting to write for it.

♥ E-mail guidelines to the list of teen contributors.

♥ Notify ten to twenty schools to work with teens within English and creative-writing classes.

As you can see, it's a big agenda, and we couldn't accomplish it if we didn't do the same thing we've proposed to you: the monthly, weekly and daily to-do lists. While we won't go into all the detail of that here, we will give you a peek at one of our weekly goal lists.

Weekly Goals: October 2–6

Monday: Meet with office staff; meet with teens at Santa Fe High School; prepare handouts for meeting with teens at Torrey Pines.

Tuesday: Edit new unit 3.

Thursday: Do Dallas media; fly home.

Just as we've recommended for you, we also have daily to-do's, an agenda that guides our activities each day. As an example:

Daily Goals: Wednesday, October 5

♥ Develop one-page overview of topics for teens wanting to write for our latest book in the *Taste Berries for Teens* series: *A Taste-Berry Teen's Guide to Setting & Achieving Goals.*

♥ Look over list of former teen contributors and potential new contributors (write, phone or e-mail teens).

♥ Notify English and creative-writing schoolteachers who wish to have their teens develop and write on select themes for new book.

♥ Begin a draft of chapter outlines for the *Goals* book.

♥ Prepare for meeting with our teen editorial review board next Monday.

♥ Set up a conference call with our publisher to determine their interest in adding a new book to the *Taste Berries for Teens* series over the next year: *A Taste-Berry Teen's Guide to Living Drug-Free.*

♥ Check to see if reservations and all plans are set for flying to Dallas on Thursday P.M. to begin book tour next day on *A Taste-Berry Teen's Guide to Managing the Stress and Pressures of Life:*

5:30 A.M.: Station: WFAA (ABC) TV Channel 8 Show: "Day Break"

7:30 A.M.: Station: KDFW (FOX) TV Channel 4 Show: "Good Day Dallas"

10:45 A.M.: Station: KLUV-Radio 98.7 FM

12:15 P.M.: Show: "Around Arlington"

3:45 P.M.: Station: A Family Net Radio—Syndicated "Master Control"
6:30 p.m.: Book-signing at Barnes and Noble, Preston & Park America West Airlines to Phoenix/change planes, arrive San Diego 10:25 P.M.

So that's the way it works in our office! As with all our goals, as we reach one, we're on to the next. As it pertains to developing books for our *Taste Berries for Teens* series, we're always planning for new books. Right now, we have several in the works, including one we feel will be helpful to teens in saying "no" to the devastating pitfalls of drug and alcohol addiction. We're also doing a book on the subject of love and another on "1001 Questions Teens Ask," as well as others. So, we have some serious—and exciting—goals ahead of us! We trust that you do, too!

As always, we look forward to hearing from you. We'd like to know ways this book was helpful to you, and any advice you have on what would make it better! And speaking of goals, we're always looking for taste-berry stories—those showing how you confronted real-life challenges and successfully moved beyond them. So, if you'd like to submit a story or a poem, please send them to us at:

Taste Berries for Teens
c/o Teen Team
3060 Racetrack View Drive, Suite #101–103
Del Mar, CA 92014

As Always, Taste Berries to You! Bettie and Jennifer Leigh Youngs

Appendix:
Worksheets

Worksheet #1: My Goals

1. **SPIRITUAL GROWTH:** What are your goals for peace of mind, search for meaning and spiritual fulfillment?

___ I'd like to: _____

_____

_____

___ I'd like to: _____

_____

_____

___ I'd like to: _____

_____

_____

2. **PERSONAL RELATIONSHIPS:** What are your goals for enhancing your relationships (with parents, friends, teachers, others)?

___ I'd like to: _____

_____

_____

___ I'd like to: _____

_____

_____

___ I'd like to: _____

_____

_____

3. **LEARNING/EDUCATION:** What would you like to know more about? What skills do you want to develop?

___ I'd like to: _____

_____

_____

___ I'd like to: _____

_____

_____

___ I'd like to: _____

_____

_____

4. **STATUS AND RESPECT:** To which groups/organizations/ associations or other affiliations do you want to belong? From whom do you want respect?

___ I'd like to: _____

_____

_____

___ I'd like to: _____

_____

_____

___ I'd like to: _____

_____

_____

5. **LEISURE/HOBBIES:** What activities (hobbies, sports, travels) would you like to learn more about (or to do more of)?

___ I'd like to: _____

_____

_____

___ I'd like to: _____

_____

_____

___ I'd like to: _____

_____

_____

6. **FITNESS/HEALTH/WELL-BEING:** What are your goals for your physical fitness and overall health?

___ I'd like to: _____

_____

_____

___ I'd like to: _____

_____

_____

___ I'd like to: _____

_____

_____

7. **FINANCIAL:** What are your goals for having enough money to do the things you want to do?

___ I'd like to: _____

_____

_____

___ I'd like to: _____

_____

_____

___ I'd like to: _____

_____

_____

8. **JOB/CAREER:** What kind of job would you like? What are your goals for productive work and career success?

___ I'd like to: _____

_____

_____

___ I'd like to: _____

_____

_____

___ I'd like to: _____

_____

_____

9. **COMMUNITY SERVICE/SERVING OTHERS:** What are your plans to do "good works" within your neighborhood and community, and to help others?

___ I'd like to: _____

_____

_____

___ I'd like to: _____

_____

_____

___ I'd like to: _____

_____

_____

Worksheet #2:
Activities I Need to Do to Meet My Goals

1. SPIRITUAL GROWTH

My Goal: _____

_____

_____

Tasks to do in meeting this goal: **Must be completed by:**

_____

_____

_____

_____

_____

_____

2. PERSONAL RELATIONSHIPS

My Goal: _____

_____

_____

Tasks to do in meeting this goal: **Must be completed by:**

_____

_____

_____

_____

_____

_____

3. **LEARNING/EDUCATION**

My Goal: _____

_____

_____

Tasks to do in meeting this goal: **Must be completed by:**

_____

_____

_____

_____

_____

_____

4. **STATUS AND RESPECT**

My Goal: _____

_____

_____

Tasks to do in meeting this goal: **Must be completed by:**

_____

_____

_____

_____

_____

_____

5. **LEISURE/HOBBIES**

My Goal: _____

_____

_____

Tasks to do in meeting this goal: **Must be completed by:**

_____

_____

_____

_____

_____

_____

_____

6. **FITNESS/HEALTH/WELL-BEING**

My Goal: _____

_____

_____

Tasks to do in meeting this goal: **Must be completed by:**

_____

_____

_____

_____

_____

_____

7. FINANCIAL

My Goal: _____

_____

_____

Tasks to do in meeting this goal: **Must be completed by:**

_____

_____

_____

_____

_____

_____

8. JOB/CAREER

My Goal: _____

_____

_____

Tasks to do in meeting this goal: **Must be completed by:**

_____

_____

_____

_____

_____

_____

9. COMMUNITY SERVICE/SERVING OTHERS

My Goal: _____

_____

_____

Tasks to do in meeting this goal: **Must be completed by:**

_____

_____

_____

_____

_____

_____

_____

Worksheet #3:
Monthly "To-Do's" in Meeting My Goals

January To-Do's   **Must be completed by:**

_____

_____

_____

_____

_____

_____

_____

_____

_____

February To-Do's   **Must be completed by:**

_____

_____

_____

_____

_____

_____

_____

_____

_____

_____

March To-Do's   **Must be completed by:**

_____

_____

_____

_____

_____

_____

_____

_____

_____

_____

April To-Do's   **Must be completed by:**

_____

_____

_____

_____

_____

_____

_____

_____

_____

_____

May To-Do's   **Must be completed by:**

_____

_____

_____

_____

_____

_____

_____

_____

_____

_____

_____

June To-Do's   **Must be completed by:**

_____

_____

_____

_____

_____

_____

_____

_____

_____

_____

July To-Do's   **Must be completed by:**

_____

_____

_____

_____

_____

_____

_____

_____

_____

_____

August To-Do's   **Must be completed by:**

_____

_____

_____

_____

_____

_____

_____

_____

_____

_____

September To-Do's   **Must be completed by:**

_____

_____

_____

_____

_____

_____

_____

_____

_____

_____

October To-Do's   **Must be completed by:**

_____

_____

_____

_____

_____

_____

_____

_____

_____

_____

November To-Do's   **Must be completed by:**

_____

_____

_____

_____

_____

_____

_____

_____

_____

_____

December To-Do's   **Must be completed by:**

_____

_____

_____

_____

_____

_____

_____

_____

_____

_____

Worksheet #4: My Weekly Goals

Goals for Week #1

_____

_____

_____

_____

_____

_____

_____

_____

_____

Goals for Week #2

_____

_____

_____

_____

_____

_____

_____

_____

_____

_____

Goals for Week #3

_____

_____

_____

_____

_____

_____

_____

_____

_____

_____

Goals for Week #4

_____

_____

_____

_____

_____

_____

_____

_____

_____

_____

Worksheet #5: My Daily "To-Do's"

Monday To-Do's

_____

_____

_____

_____

_____

_____

_____

_____

Tuesday To-Do's

_____

_____

_____

_____

_____

_____

_____

_____

Wednesday To-Do's

_____

_____

_____

_____

_____

_____

_____

_____

_____

Thursday To-Do's

_____

_____

_____

_____

_____

_____

_____

_____

_____

Friday To-Do's

_____

_____

_____

_____

_____

_____

_____

_____

_____

Weekend To-Do's

_____

_____

_____

_____

_____

_____

_____

_____

_____

Worksheet #6:
Removing the Obstacles to Meeting My Goals

Goal: _____

_____

STEP #1: What obstacle stands in the way of my achieving my goal?

♥ Obstacle: _____

_____

STEP #2: What can I do to remove this obstacle?

I could: _____

_____

I could: _____

_____

I could: _____

_____

STEP #3: Do I need help removing this obstacle and, if so, who can I ask and specifically, what will I ask of that person?

I will ask _____ to help me by _____

_____

_____

I will ask _____ to help me by _____

_____

_____

About the Authors

Bettie B. Youngs, Ph.D., Ed.D., is a Pulitzer Prize–nominated author of twenty-one books translated into thirty-one languages. She is a former Teacher-of-the-Year, university professor and executive director of Instruction and Professional Development, Inc. A long-acknowledged expert on teen issues, Dr. Youngs has frequently appeared on *The Good Morning Show, NBC Nightly News*, CNN, *Oprah* and *Geraldo. USA Today*, the *Washington Post, Redbook, McCall's, U.S. News & World Report, Working Woman, Family Circle, Parents, Better Homes & Gardens, Woman's Day* and the National Association for Secondary School Principals (NASSP) have all recognized her work. Her acclaimed books include: *Taste Berries for Teens: Inspirational Short Stories and Encouragement on Life, Love, Friendship and Tough Issues; Safeguarding Your Teenager from the Dragons of Life; How to Develop Self-Esteem in Your Child; You and Self-Esteem: A Book for Young People; Taste-Berry Tales;* the Pulitzer Prize–nominated *Gifts of the Heart: Stories That Celebrate Life's Defining Moments;* and the award-winning *Values from the Heartland.* Dr. Youngs is the author of a number of videocassette programs and is the co-author of the nationally acclaimed Parents on Board, a video-based training program to help schools and parents work together to increase student achievement.

Jennifer Leigh Youngs, twenty-seven, is a speaker and work-shop presenter for teens and parents nationwide. She is the author of *Feeling Great, Looking Hot & Loving Yourself! Health,*

Fitness and Beauty for Teens; and coauthor of *Taste Berries for Teens: Inspirational Short Stories and Encouragement on Life, Love, Friendship and Tough Issues; Taste Berries for Teens Journal; More Taste Berries for Teens; A Taste-Berry Teen's Guide to Managing the Stress and Pressures of Life;* and *Taste Berries for Teens #3: Inspirational Stories and Encouragement on Life, Love, Friends and the Face in the Mirror.* Jennifer is a former Miss Teen California finalist and Rotary International Goodwill Ambassador and Exchange Scholar. She serves on a number of advisory boards for teens and is a Youth Coordinator for Airline Ambassadors, an international organization affiliated with the United Nations that involves youth in programs to build cross-cultural friend-ships; escorts children to hospitals for medical care and orphans to new homes; and delivers humanitarian aid to those in need worldwide.

To contact Bettie B. Youngs or Jennifer Leigh Youngs, write to:

Youngs, Youngs & Associates
3060 Racetrack View Drive
Del Mar, CA 92014

Inspiration and Guidance

Code #5475 • $11.95

Read about people who make a difference in the lives of others. By their examples, these individuals will show you how to use your daily life to improve the world you live in and the lives of others.

Code #4193 • $11.95

Gifts of the Heart will show you that small miracles can and will take place in your everyday life.

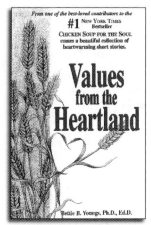

Code #3359 • $11.95

The beautiful and poignant stories from *Values from the Heartland* will help you discover the deeper side of integrity, commitment, honor, self-discipline, connection and character.

Also from Bettie
and Jennifer Leigh Youngs

Code #6692 • $12.95

Code #7680 • $12.95

Find the encouragement and support you need in this innovative collection of inspirational short stories on life, love and friendship. The journal has been created as an excellent companion giving you plenty of space for writing about your feelings and experiences.